What a magnificent work of Spirit! Treva McLean (The Basic Humanity Handbooks) goes straight to the core of True Self to unearth profound insight and knowings of the Self to be One, Perfect, Harmonious Whole – imbued with intrinsic, divine ability to heal from hurt, separation, anxiety, and isolation.

The Basic Humanity Handbooks offers manifold tools of spirit that can help you reclaim joy, abundance, and harmony by remembering who you are.

> Bri Maya Tiwari
> Vedic Monk
> Wise Earth Monastery
> February 6, 2002

The Basic Humanity Handbooks
PHASE ONE

LEVEL ONE:
THE DIVINEMENTS
THE DIVINITY KEY CODES

TREVA MCLEAN

©2002 Basic Humanity Ink, Inc.

All Rights Reserved.
Without limiting the rights under copyright reserved above,
no part of this publication may be reproduced, stored in or introduced
into a retrieval system, or transmitted, in any form or by any means
(electronic, mechanical, photocopying, recording, or otherwise),
without the prior written permission of both the copyright owner
and the publisher of this book.

Published by Basic Humanity Ink, Inc.

Basic Humanity Ink, Inc.
9649 Highway 105 South – Box 5101, Banner Elk, NC USA 28604

PaperBack Edition
ISBN 0-9717554-0-X

Design, Editing, Typography by Deborah Mayhall Bradshaw
Valle Crucis, NC USA 28691

Text set in Goudy
Printed at Inové Graphics, Kingsport, TN, USA

TABLE OF CONTENTS

Divinements One through Eight
    Divine Align 5
    Divine Home 9
    Divine Father 13
    Divine Mother 17
    Divine Desire 21
    Divine Health 25
    Divine Breath 29
    Divine Manifestation 33

Divinements Nine Through Sixteen
    Divine Relating 39
    Divine Allowance 43
    Divine Attraction 47
    Divine Cell-a-bration .51
    Divine Worth 55
    Divine Surrender 59
    Divine Family 63
    Divine Faith 67

Divinements Seventeen through Twenty-four
    Divine Will 73
    Divine Mind 77
    Divine Deserving 81
    Divine Motivation 85
    Divine Esteem 89
    Divine Strength 93
    Divine Learning 97
    Divine Intuition 101

Divinements Twenty-five through Thirty-two
    Divine Love 107
    Divine Peace 111
    Divine Compassion .115
    Divine Sharing 119
    Divine Harmony 123
    Divine O-Mission 127
    Divine Delight 131
    Divine Rest 135

Divinements Thirty-Three through Forty
    Divine Communication 141
    Divine Revealing 145
    Divine Listening 149
    Divinely Speaking .153
    Divinely Words For-Giving 157
    Divinely Worded Living 161
    Divinely Praises Ringing 165
    Divine Design 169

Divinements Forty-three through Forty-eight
    Divine Light 175
    Divine Knowing 179
    Divine Brow-sing .183
    Divine Attention .187
    Divine Intention .191
    Divine Integration 195
    Divine I AM 199
    Divine Meditation 202

Divinements Forty-nine through Fifty-six
    Divine On-Line 209
    Divine Dessert 213
    Divine Communication 217
    Divine Non-mind .221
    Divine Synchronicity 225
    Divine Time 229
    Divine Essence 233
    Divine Divine 237

Divinements Fifty-seven through Sixty-four
    Divine Humanity .243
    Divine Author 247
    Divine Energy 251
    Divine Bell 255
    Divine Birthday 259
    Divine Marriage 263
    Divine Authority .267
    Divine In-Light-enment 271

Basic Humanity Handbook
Phase One / Level One

THE DIVINEMENTS
The Divinity Key Codes

The curriculum for
Basic Humanity Ink, Inc. is
written in 64 phases . . .

This is One.
Light. Love. Life. All continuums . . .
with segments much like minutes,
of a greater whole, like an hour,
expressing the multiplicity
of a "One" . . .

I leave you with this,
the lightest choice,
called Basic Humanity . . .

I have been given a gift –
the gentle gift of remembering who I am
and an ancient technique for the
effective management of the "mind" of the body.

Simply said, You are divine.
You are divinity, deity, and the One's daily delight.

Within the framework of the
Power of the Law of One
there issues forth a decree:
Know thyself and be free –

HERE'S THE KEY.

You are DIVINE and thereby heir to certain spirit – inherent qualities, the divinements. I am here to remind you and to encourage you to remember what you know . . . to remember to reactivate these divinements using a simple technique . . . this is our goal. This technique, once activated, can be used in infinite and astonishingly varied application(s).

This handbook is written in eight helpful sections. At the beginning of each section you will find a list of the eight divinements pertinent to that level.

Feel freed to move lightly through this book. Your order of reading is exactly the perfect one for you. Trust yourself, your cells, and your soul. They are all one light leading the way. Home in. The symbols which resonate remain in the infinity to infinity wave of your frame.

Look at each symbol, read the remarks, follow the feelings felt straight in your heart. Know that the Symbol is a part of the whole. Load it with meaning and embrace with your soul. Flood your entire being with love's DIVINE crystal light. The spark is now flaming. Follow the footprints with the eyes of your soul. Sixty-four symbols later you are ABSOLUTELY HOME.

THE DIVINEMENTS

KEY CODES 1 - 8

DIVINE ALIGN
DIVINE HOME
DIVINE FATHER
DIVINE MOTHER
DIVINE DESIRE
DIVINE HEALTH
DIVINE BREATH
DIVINE MANIFESTATION

DIVINE ALIGN / Will-to-live

You choose to be here, in this life, at this time, in this body. Align yourself with the divine design and know that you made all the decisions . . . where, when, how, to whom, with whom . . . you are the creator and the created, a part of the One and one of the many – You were, and are, willing to be here in this magnificent world at this magnificent time.

ALIGN.
WILL.
LIVE.

The creator and the created. It's you, you choose the time, the place, your own point of entry. Enjoy the knowledge that you made the decisions as part of the grand plan/design. Wake up as designed and see the truth that ALIGNMENT is also a part of your choice – free will – free your will to lift your delight full heart to the point and the place of LIGHTEST surrender, DIVINEST love, where were you when your LIGHT was born? The spark of the infinite is the dress that you wore and the smile mirrored back is the slap of your jeaned retreat, the dancing ALIGNMENT of your elevated feet, the Christos has blended with Buddhic belief to point now an arrow at the lip of this seat and swinging delicately is the brightest ALIGNMENT, the absolute balance, the perfect escape to the central portal of all embrace. You are the LIGHTEST man I know as you surrender your knees to the bending relief of the blend I call Free and Will. Will you be free? By design? Just ALIGN. Divinely. Intimately. Intimately I AM free to be the Divinity and the LIGHT-filled lover that I AM. I AM enticed by your return to the line directly beneath and within and above the perfect love – the deepest seat – Have a rest at the point of bliss, the place of munificent taste and magnetic North. The tip called NOW at the apex of the pyramid called Solar Plexian view. The news? Know your mind. The entire 90% often considered less than the common 10. I am within the spine of Divine align. Know the book called you. Let us bless the release of the muttering head. I am lead by the gut of my instinctive walk . . . homeward . . . still . . . to DIVINE ALIGN.

DIVINE FORM

Deep in the core of your C-elf, your cellular self, lies a complete pattern of the being you are here to discover into being fully alive. Watering your cells, your soul, with the emotion of the knowing of your divinity, your divine nature, you are washed clear – free to sample the infinity of home and homeward simultaneously. Home lies within the crystal love of your pure heart. Home lies within the freedom of discovering the expanse of the universe, of the infinite kingdom, of the glorious heaven which lies within your own soul, your own full dwelling heart of simply spoken divine love.

CRYSTAL FORM
CRYSTAL HOME
CRYSTAL BODY
Dwell within and know the expanse . . .
of you.

Bless this mess, the perfect retreat. This waking dream I call the golden street. I AM writing to your tender heart from the lip of this hook I call where my hats look best on the rack beside my humble bed. Let emotion roar her way through 80% of my hectic day. I am led HOMEWARD . . . still . . . by the kindest hand . . . my own . . . leading HOME to the heart of this matter. Welling forth to clear my path, to close my door, to offer more within the shore of sweet remembrance. I am HOME by DIVINE design and I dance upon the lip of my waving express, my swirling dress of elegant swell spinning on moon's beamed countenanced telling of the softest story, the return of glory, the love of Mother, the strength of Father. I am HOME to love the other as myself, full of brother-hood and LIGHT to the middle. Know more should, see the bless of living your LIGHT at this holy address. The bears of bitter grind have moved to the north to live in the white and the tears of the Mother, dried, drip no more and you my gentle savior have walked through my door and I know more in the heart of this matter's return to the Bliss that I AM. I AM whole and healed and I know your hand as well as my own, and we are both known by an energy now owned in fullest embrace. Sailing HOME to the face I know best, my Father's place here in the eyes called my own. Let us speak of the DIVINITY made form. Meet the taste of HOME smacking wet and ambrosial and rich on the lips of our twining embrace with the race we call man. Human. Basic. DIVINE. HOME.

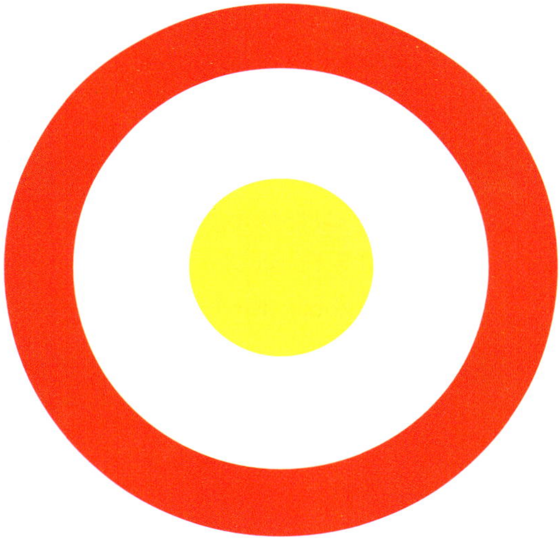

DIVINE FATHER

You are divinely male whether in the female form or the male form. Appendages and hormones and chemicals aside, at your core you are divine – divinely spirit, divinely God – divinely taking your chosen form "suit" and embracing the strength of knowing pursuit, of knowing the penetrating truth, of knowing the entry of spirit into the flesh. Know your power, embrace the tower which your right-sided, left-minded spirit piercing the veil of the form provides. Stand in it. Grasp this opportunity fully and take the lead. Divinely lead by the strength of your own hand. You are the man – enjoy the foundation of the male – you can bank on this reserve of solid inner strength.

My FATHER'S fine and knows the line of fasten-ating return to the zipperless ledge called my spine and I am entendered with the prodigal return, the expert experience of tunneling within to the heartline called mine. And I know the balance of truth full encounter with the power of the hour quartered by four to reveal the expatriate, 15 times more than the nesting partner I call the shore of remember and the office of trust and the articles of hush at the place called the burst of intrigue and the element called me. True to form. I'm getting warm within the springs of generating seams. Welcome to the lifetime I call living the dreamless life to benefit the scheme of the FATHER'S regime. Know the name. Guard the find. I call it me. Home to stay. It's nature's way. All one dream and the penetrating scheme of our eternal forever. Love the FATHER. Fill the seam. Life's begun within the sun of FATHER'S finest. Hours. Ours. Forever. FATHER DIVINE.

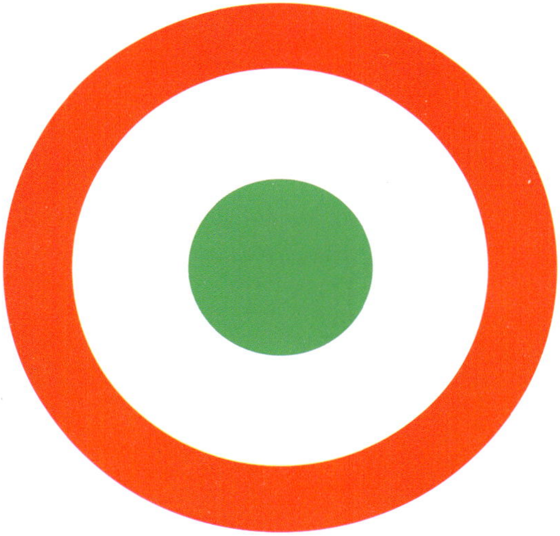

DIVINE MOTHER

Divinely female, you are purely intuitive and receptive to the in pouring power of your divine male carrying home the rewards of the spirit. Knowing this, you sense the need and make the space for the soft influx of the seed of the spirit – you nurture the truth of the delightful knowledge and laugh with pride at the sensitive, left-handed, right-minded sort of knowing which whispers softly – you are Divine. Divinely you. Divinely freed male. Divinely female . . . Receptive and deep.

MOTHER, you are the lover, the giver and the life, the welcome in the middle which we call insight to the ocean of 78 parts wet and gentle to exposure, the elements are set to ring the tidings, to this, our story tell of the lifting light exposure of this infinite hotel. The rooms are all-ways lighted and the hallways are the spark of deepest delving climbing to the MOTHER that you are. The womb of cavey dewey is moist upon my face as I enter knowing loving is the mantra of this place. I am alive within the space of the MOTHER'S deep embrace, moist the taste, manna honeyed pasty flour of feeding plenty. Know the hour of being twenty to the 13th and the Mayan knowing spread. We are now the showing and we've nine to four to tread tripping on the light arc to the loving receiving spread. I am aligned with the will to recline in sweet surrender to the MOTHER I remember. Well. Let us tell the story, fullest glory. LIGHT, on the inside, where in founts in flowing knowing, on the inside molten glowing, whispering showing of galactic flowing to the cleft of the rock, the space in place for the great cosmic shift. Know the *God in you, know that you are, the beatific view, the taste of the space flourite lined to bosom's too fine to mention in less than one breath, one hu-man-ity being born, the hour 13 has come into view in the womb of the MOTHER, the loving other, is it true – humanity's spool of webbing proof, the blanket energetic directs the leafy flow of the quad-seasonal knowing that your divinity is showing.
The MOTHER lode, the earth your own. DIVINELY sister. Know the MOTHER. DIVINE MOTHER.

*Defined simply here, the greatest energetic resource.

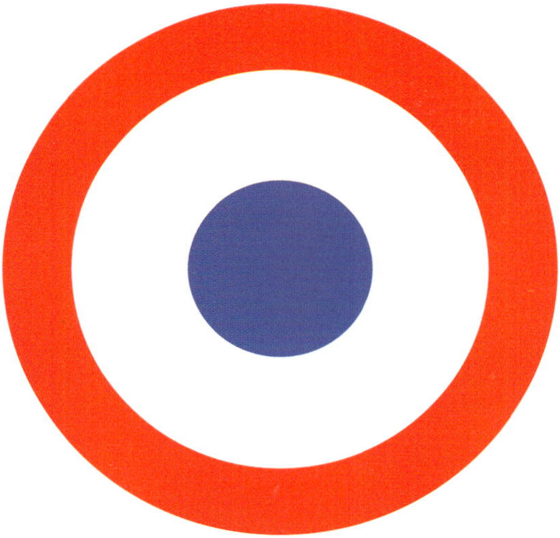

DIVINE DESIRE

Divinely desire to light the magnetic, swirling inferno of creative living passion which wells forth from the root of your being. Delight in the divinity of the swelling, surging, flaming knowing that we are One with the Cosmic Creator. We are One and the One silvery burning violet-red flame of the deep yearning desire to know the melting moment when we remember our original ignition and we burn our way through to the truth and the light of knowing our heart's
burning return to the sparkling crystal torch
of Divine Desire . . .

Know the Power.
Create Your Life.
Standing Fire.

It is my DIVINE DESIRE to bless this meal, this banquet called life, with the peaceable entreaty of a light living needy to plug herself in to the living again. I am welcome to feel the enchanting thrill of my spirit warming to the stretch of another year's growing flight, span to span. I am DIVINE within the structure of my centered trip to the tip of infinity's arrival to the sparking revival and within my triple star-sided expression of the circling square lifted effortlessly and evidently to the expulsion of energy lift to right the balancing needle, compass pointed due North, to the brinking lip of summer's trip to the land of greenest dawn and the lap of moonbeams brushes the laughter home again and my magnetic desire draws this portrait's increase as the fullness of my adult stand, my divinity's span is ignited arc to arc, heaven to heart to heavenly spark, one arcing band, optional, essential, and welcome to blend in the apostolic epistle most sincere, my own name written soft upon my whispering heart, welcome home little spark, know the light most DIVINE, feel the spine of this book called you and enjoy the spin of living again. Healthy and heartfelt and free, I am me. The most desirable blend of the three. The earth's tree of knowledge spread and expansive and gifted entrance to the land of remember by DIVINE design and absolutely ecstatic, emphatic DIVINEST DESIRE. Let us recline in resting anticipation of DIVINE health, as DESIRED.
DIVINE DESIRE.

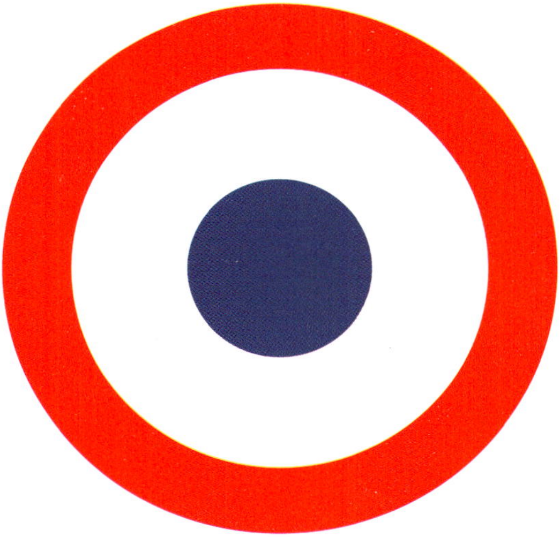

DIVINE HEALTH

Dance the dance of Divinity in form. Fill your pockets with the polish of a life well-balanced, gently blended to include the elements, minerals, vitamins, self-loving, spirit-led body, soul, and mind trusting walk which leads you softly through the layers of neglect and abuse to the glorious oasis of balanced dental, mental, emotional, physical, familial, spiritual, and yes you can have all of yourself operating at maximum bliss with minimum fuss. Tune in to your bodies and turn up the intuition knob by trusting your knowing and grow whole-y well.

DIVINE HEALTH. I am seeking, the balance and the space of columns wide with lifting harmonious gifted return to the well-spent showing light-filled employee of exactly what I am on the inside. Anatomically speaking and ergonomically swelling, I am telling my truth and living my proof and seeking my spirit in singular cells and feeling the surrender to the living dance, the billowing attend called imminent, immediate immaculate and well . . . I am living to tell, to articulate, to say that my light-loving heart is home to stay melting deep and rich and brilliant in red-green retreat to the blue lipped escape to the window of greatest wealth my living, loving, blue-green ecstatic enigmatic, smiling leap to the top of this life's peace-full blender of velvet smooth flowing arrival. DIVINELY spoken, I am, and God has chosen to be imaged by me. A snapshot of perfect HEALTH – just one breath away from a lifetime of dusty delay. *Aloha. Know the art of breathing safe into the place of perfect space – the pinnacle is near. Wearing well. Let me tell you about my living penetration of the eloquent art of total regeneration. Let it be. DIVINE HEALTH and ME. In one sweeping inhalation of the God in me. Cell to cell, I am well. Oh sweet and tender.
DIVINE HEALTH.

*Aloha: Hawaiian greeting. Hello & good bye in the presence of the breath, yours and mine.

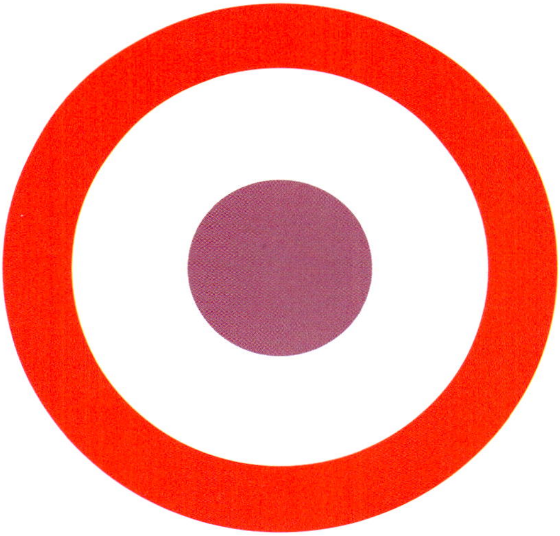

DIVINE BREATH

Breath of life. Breathe yourself full. Fill the sails of your soul with the deep, cell feeding, being, of breathing the divine breath. In the moment, know the depth of the truth that awareness to the in and out, the filling up, the ebbing out the making space, the filling in, will lend to your divinity. Deeply breathing, you are swollen with the knowledge that air, oxygen, and you are sharing this moment and you are breathing great gulps of God . . . whether there's awareness of the breathing we call life, is up to you. Know the Divine breath and know the depths of your own Divinity.

BREATHE me home on a sparkling line of milky way time, tapping away at the resistance in me. Setting free the breathing tree, the living branch, the flowering chance called DIVINITY. In one twinkling nod, I am acknowledged by a star tipping her veil just one blink too near and tiny body blundering topples shimmering and simply exactly on-line with the inside of my being BREATHING. BREATHE the welcome with your brother. There's no "Other" less than near to exactly this minute of lulling you. Breathe just a minute, the thorough essence, feel it filling your lifting with be-ing internal and monumentally direct, the tower, the column, the lightest interject is you in the middle, light rhythmic, and desired by infinite air for the journey inside. Cleanse your temple, your many mitochondrial, through your breathing revival of the DIVINITY in you. Know your BREATH. Your every step. It's all DIVINE within the line of sweet and tender breathing surrender. I AM DIVINE. BREATHE me in. Kissing God.
An ecstacy direct from the DIVINE BREATH.

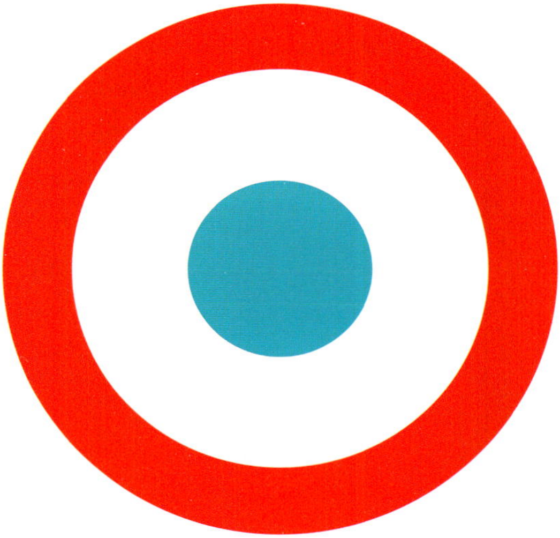

DIVINE MANIFESTATION

Drawing the life that I desire to me with my
clearly intended design for the highest good,
I am filled with knowing the compassionate art
of divine manifestation. Gratefully walking,
I am led to pencil in the knowing agreement to
be fully aware in my creating splendor and I
surrender to the notion that heart knows best
and trusting my Divinity I draw myself home to
the life I have chosen. I co-create with every
inch of our being and I rejoice in the knowing
that my manifestations are showing and that
yours interface, divinely laced, divinely
manifested, Divinely held, fully accepted
and graciously. We are Divine.

MANIFESTLY made by the gentle hand, the loving entreaty, the politically grand and sweeping gesture. The uplifting spark, the beneficial sound of a whispering lark. Know the word. Know the light of DIVINITY in sight. Create your path with energy that lasts in perfect reflection of your crystal clear intention. Exceed invention. Be the patent. You are your best product. The earth you are on it and for lasting profit, for all concerned become elastic and feed your gastric juices with light filled droplets of breathing sensation, tasting this nation, this national treasure, this absolute manifestation of waving pleasure. Breathe in the name most holy, most sacred, your own. And know the leisure of the clearest temple, your own, home to the one, your laughing sum, of the penetrating ray that leads you home to play in the lake of crystal reflection. See your light, know your path. Share your truth and make your own splash in the pool of crystalline DIVINE MANIFESTATION. Creation's near. Know the power and the place of taking a response-able position, right in the center of you. DIVINE MANIFESTATION.

THE DIVINEMENTS

KEY CODES 9 - 16

DIVINE RELATING

DIVINE ALLOWANCE

DIVINE ATTRACTION

DIVINE CELL-A-BRATION

DIVINE WORTH

DIVINE SURRENDER

DIVINE FAMILY

DIVINE FAITH

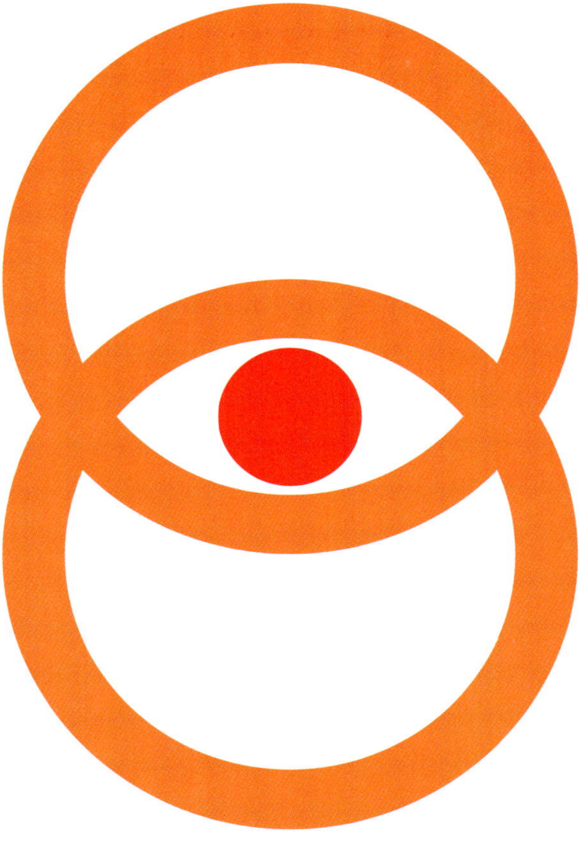

DIVINE RELATING

Related to this moment's walk, I am reminded of the reality that the golden ruler of friendship measured lies in the heart of my desire to hold myself wholly Divine and wholly worthy of my complete acceptance of my desire to treat you, your heart, your desires as absolutely Divine and absolutely worthy of my highest regard. The gift offered is my unconditional honesty in relation to our shared desires. I am complete, full - filling and eternally open to the highest self regard and the deepest immersion of crystal clear communication and to the pure absolute of our connection. I love you as, and to, the extent that I love myself. I am divine, you are divine. Let us entwine in the rest-full assurance of our divine relation.

RELATING to the space, I am equal to the taste of sweet surrender's ambrosial place at the roof of our rotted exposure to race related circumpolar anticipation and knowing the temptation of sharing the station that I call me with you. I am filling the tank of RELATIVE persuasion with the coy notion that straight up devotion spoken direct is the subtlest arrow shot straight to the heart of DIVINE RELATING. I am mating my self with the highest wealth, the fondest collection of expectant association with the in-fact-uation called communicating about relating. I know the glow of chatting through evenings of certain entreaty and expulsive hushes met with the face of a turquoise embrace and I am the infant living at places of silvery uniform winging flights appropriate to the humble adoration DIVINE and I am the lifting, the gifting energetic, the loving kinetic called absolute bliss. Welcome to the platter of loving the matter as hearts feel welcoming hearts, like their own. I am the rhythm and the patter and the tribute and the yellow-green icing of the lift called enticing, and I am with you my spirit, my friend, my infinite other. My elegance sends me sailing to the peace of knowing our penetrating conversation has met the wedge of pi-ing return to spine out the web of insight-full intrigue with seeing the other in my mirrored reflection of the DIVINITY in you. DIVINE RELATING. Truth to tell. You are DIVINE and RELATIVE to me, let us entwine in DIVINE RELATING.

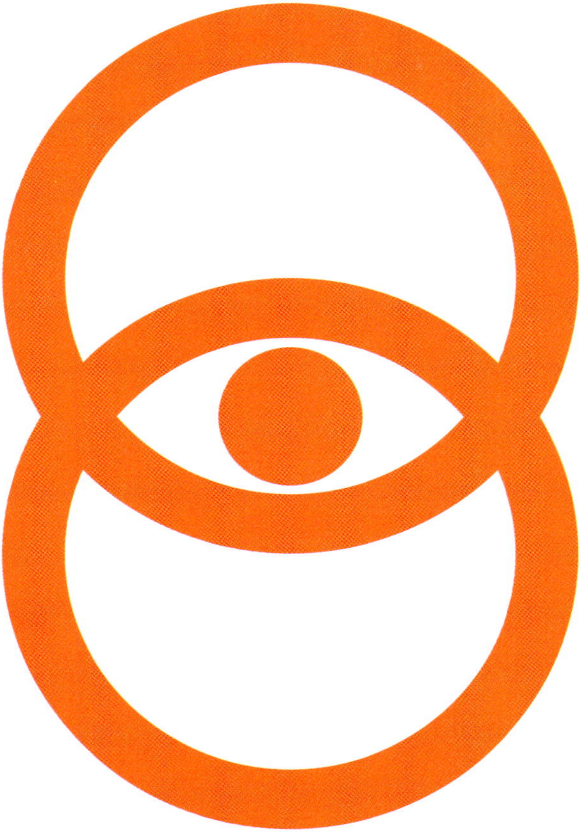

DIVINE ALLOWANCE

The allotment of an allowance is my knowing that in writing you a Divine permission slip to be perfectly imperfectly Divine, that I am gifting myself with the precise freedom which I have offered to you, my Divine and perfect mirror of just how gracious, accepting, understanding, and kind I am to myself. Let us embrace the ancient knowing way of love without expectation and manipulation, without motive and without the conditional. I love you unconditionally with the divine understanding that we walk the same path, in the same shoes, with the same need for Divine allowance, for Divine self-permission to fulfill our purpose – to joyfully express ourselves fully. Divine Self-Love turns the key to full allowance of our peaceful expression of perfection.

Let us allow our delicate selves to meet at the table called tender surrender and allow our acknowledgement of the intrepid far gone and the trailing star of a comet gone home. At the brink of deliverance, I marry my self to the light far DIVINEST and the welcome called wealth. I'm attracted to the beauty, the infinite link, the circling in-spiral to the planet called me. I am DIVINE and enlivened by the opportunity to allow the return of the father called DIVINE. Let us trace the embrace upon the sky of the genuine face mirrored wet with tear-y healing of the deserving ignition, for the light has become my healing friend, patient and trim to the sail set within on the lake of my intimate swim with the DIVINE I AM. A swan worn thin by ducking refusal to blend within, is a swan once again upon receiving greeting, billing, wooing, cooing home to the absolute again by DIVINE ALLOWANCE.

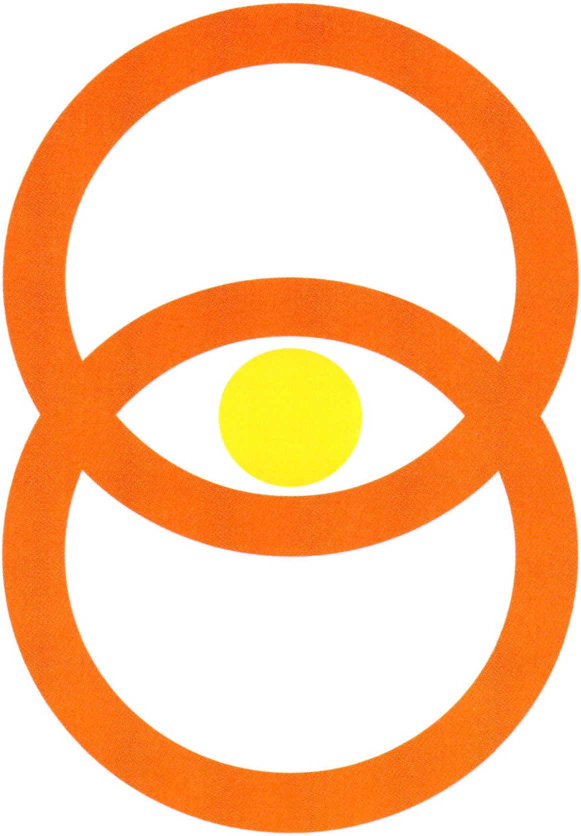

DIVINE ATTRACTION

In the gentle light of your expectant hush,
I know the beauty of our shared desire for
absolute and complete reunion and communion
with the convocation we call full-immersion
with the beloved. Your divinity shines forth
casting a soft glowing shadow which mingles with
and pulsates with the magnetic desire of our
shared remembrance. Loving you is loving me.
Knowing you, I remember us and I know that the
Divine shines in your face and heart, and willing
to reveal and desiring desire's completion, I
anticipate our union, our return to the whole
piece of the no longer puzzling pie and I desire to
draw us both to the center stage of our shared
fascination with the God we are and we are
magnetically one.

Attentive to me, I'm watching my Energetic community, my immunity has swollen to include the attraction of giving myself active attention and honestly bending to notice the crossing linear affirmations at the effortless leaning I call desirous attention to the contribution of the light acquisition called letting me see that the impasse called blocking is the tree without leaves and the truth of this matter is that living intrigues me to question, to wonder, to seek, to draw attention to me as the DIVINEST ATTRACTION, the God I call me, holy free, gentle to the middle, I am the light pyramid lifting home to smell the taste of energy swirling in a pattern complete with creative splendor like the veins of a leaf, spreading home to know the seam of quartzite dreams, granite seen, living views of nitrogen's fire and willowy blue attraction leads to action's firey adaptation of the living nation, the welcome kin, the family's friend is the only infiltration, the without hesitation return to the heart called my own. By DIVINE ATTRACTION. I am shone the intricately simply path to my home eternally led by DIVINE ATTRACTION.

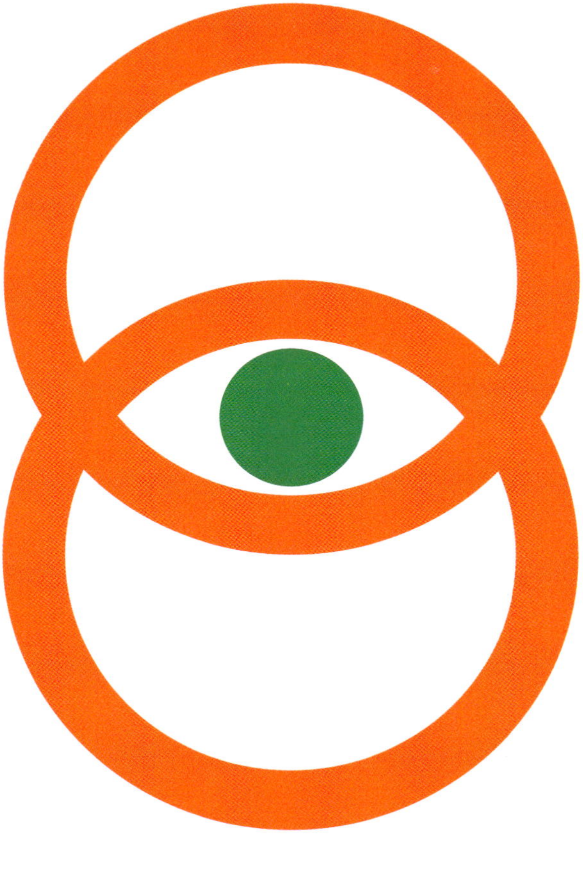

DIVINE CELL-A-BRATION (JOY)

Joyfully expressive, my cells swirl with the definition of the blissful twirling dance, with the fruition of the knowing pattern, the grains of Divinity set deep within the mitochondrial mix of energetic emergence and the energy speaks and sparks with the joy of jumping feet, soul, and heart first into the glowing orange coals and shuffling our simmering into the pounding, pouring, dripping, pulsing, inferno of passionate loving dancing, glorious, joyful celebration. We empty the blocking limitations of mental constructs in one searing realization, one burning knowing of the Divine dance, the cell deep magical cell-a-bration and we soar joyfully free, winging home to cell-a-brate our liberation.

Cell to cell and wide to the middle, I am the central life-bearing adventure, the gentle reminder that the creator is kinder when I live the intention that I am the pleasurable experience of a mitochondrial intrigue with the dynamic species I AM. Human and kind, graciously respect-full, I know the triumphant delivery of the limitless recovery,the experiential, philosophic, philanthropic splendor of knowing the constellation, the internalization of keeping the peace-full intention most clear, that there is light-filled DIVINITY spoken, hear. And often I am welcome and welcome I am found to be the fondest memory of a life spent placing cards upon the table and napkins at the door, at the plate of sweet surrender, I am opening up for sure. The flood of lightest ecstacy is filling up my skin. I am the grandest design of all the laughing, singing, harmonic entreaty in calling me from within. I am joyous in my CELL-A-BRATION of the metabolic formula for absolute perfection, bliss-full acknowledge of the world's finest college, the DIVINE CELL-A-BRATION. *ATP. Mitochondria Energy and me, it's DIVINE to see the CELL-A-BRATION.

* *The energetic source by the sea, inside me. Adenosine tri-phosphate.*

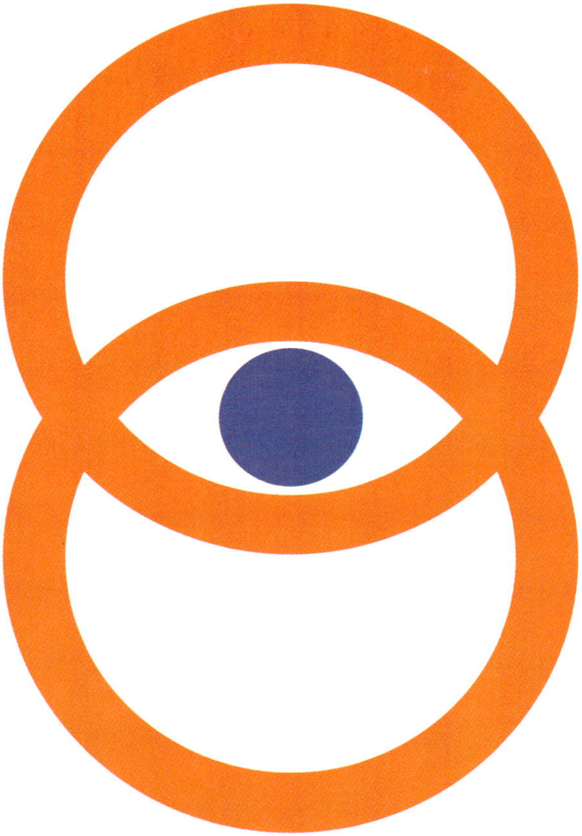

DIVINE WORTH

We are Divinity's finest creation, sparks of the Divine, pieces of God – molded from the clay of life, filled eternally with the Divine breath, we are complete, full, and absolutely, irreplaceably unique and also absolutely irreplaceably the same.

As I value myself, I value your tremendous wealth of knowing embrace and I am holy and acceptable to my divinely ruled measurement of infinite to infinite value and I hold myself worthy and I deem myself and all that you claim as your own worthy and we meet in the remembered, centered, impeccable embrace of two souls called home to the golden, sunny shore of honoring, fair, upholding integrity-laden truth of your intrinsic Divine Worth.

WORTHY.
IMPECCABLE.
VALUED.

What is it worth, this experience called birth and entering the earth? I'm healthy and happy and DIVINE in my wealth of inherent infinity and delicate worth. DIVINITY'S showing in my intimate knowing of the intellect's glowing body point indication of the heart I've been chasing, found my own, carry home on a milky chest of ancient bless pointing the path which is truest at last. Sacred tree, highest sea, glowing orb of creative flow, held to glow, in my grace full bands, a glittering disc of heart's melting drip, caught here within the grip of an influential trip to the absolute creative, central port of all mesmerizing Mayan timing. Kun, baktun, metallic cooking spoons, dipping, piquant and plenti-full at the crystalline shore of the beach front cottage with the aquamarine door and rubies of beauty sparkle at the sight of my eye-full example of trilling voice leading to the blessing called knowing that my DIVINE is showing. I am free to know the DIVINE WORTH of me seeing you, glowing through the golden grain of precious sight. I am the flight and the winged hope of DIVINITY's truth, the living proof of be-ing free and well willed with blessed serenity in the bosom of lifting shining to see the DIVINE WORTH of me.

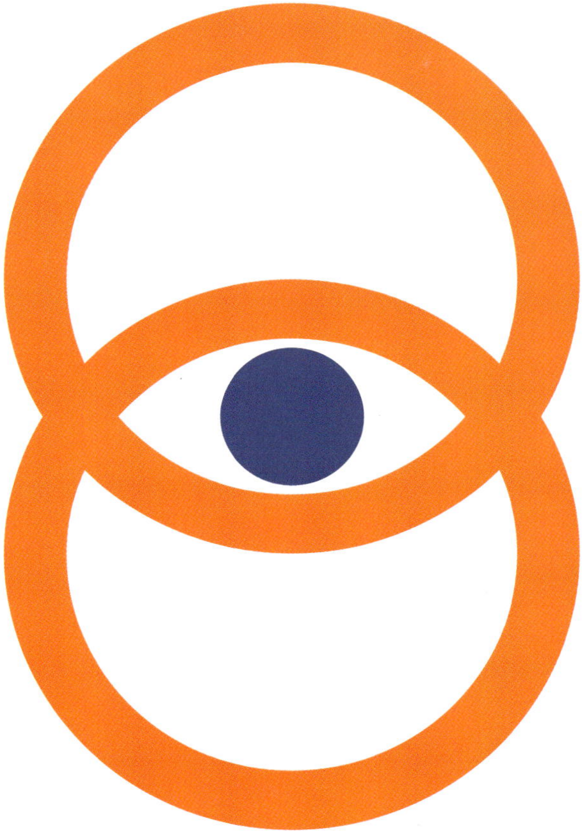

DIVINE SURRENDER

Remembering the Way In, we know the Way Out and Without Surrendering In we wander without thinking about Giving, thinking about Receiving . . . Surrender to the knowing that the only way out is all the way in . . . Accept the free flow, swim in the memory of the blood held recall carrying swirling red and white stripes of cellular Knowing. Cast off the ropes, untie the perfect Knots, unravel the cords and slip into the stream of Divine Surrender. You are the one floating above the Cosmic fishhook which snags the lessons without interrupting your drifting, swirling, rippling home to that continual, centripetal, enduring moment to moment to one ecstatic eternal Divine Surrender.

I Surrender ALL.

SURRENDER the experience and the place of just knowing, to the remembrance of bliss and the DIVINITY of showing celtic knotting, spiraling slotting of enthusiastic delivery of the living allowance to the lifting introduction, the attendant observation that there's power inflation of the billowing sail called living LIGHT well. DIVINE the line to approximate the sign of the ascendant estate called the plantation's place. Arrange the time, experience the fine art of lifting the blocks to the loving rainbow of an oracle's sort to sort out the willows, the river, the wind, to green golden apples living love's sound. I AM inclined to joy-fully recline in the welcome design of the sweet surrender called DIVINITY'S giver, one and the same us, the One called my name. This one that I am, this delicate band of spectrum wide encounter with the holy hand painting pictures full ecstatic in the sand of eternal timing. Left to remember the serenity of DIVINITY'S sweetest family. All are one, in the eternal sun of 100 waking days at the edge of the place called Delphic splendor. Be the sender of the grandest message, the loving letter, of, DIVINE SURRENDER.

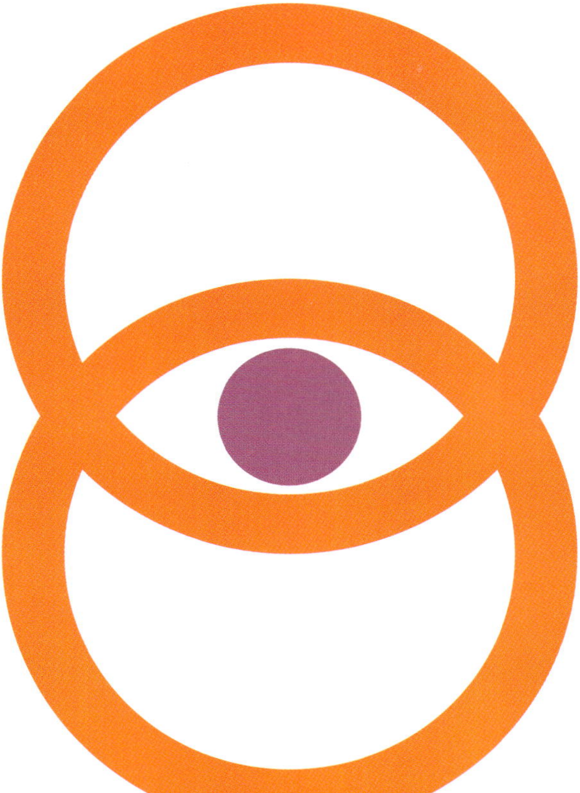

DIVINE FAMILY

Divinely membered we remember the moment of original connection and we are fascinated with the fastening love which draws us heart to heart toward the center of the eternal space called home and gathering near we remember the stories held dear and we create our chosen family of soul, our divine family . . . our family of the eternal moment. You are my sister, brother, divine father, mother – as we claim our entirety we are afforded the ever-present opportunity to sit at the head of our own table and to actively select family rather than to passively react to family given. Given this knowing, we are reminded that Divinely we chose also this family of the form and forgiveness pours full into the space called wholly acceptable and we are God and divine and family . . . all One and One All.

SISTER.
BROTHER.
MOTHER.
FATHER.
DIVINE FAMILY.

DIVINITY is my family, and brother, this includes the lovely growing experience of infinity grounded by two eternal essences, the ones I call mine and the shining one radiating here is the one I call dear, for whom I am belling and telling the thrilling, the absolute filling, the accentuated experience of the sister I AM and in the allowance of physical prowness, of peaking excellence, of genetic electives is the electrical news that you are family too.
For the DIVINITY in you is the DIVINITY in me and within the arc is the spark of sweet remember and I AM entendered with the brilliant experience of seeing and hearing and feeling the ceiling high experience of seeing the view past just three the four to the beauti-full shore of One happy DIVINE FAMILY.

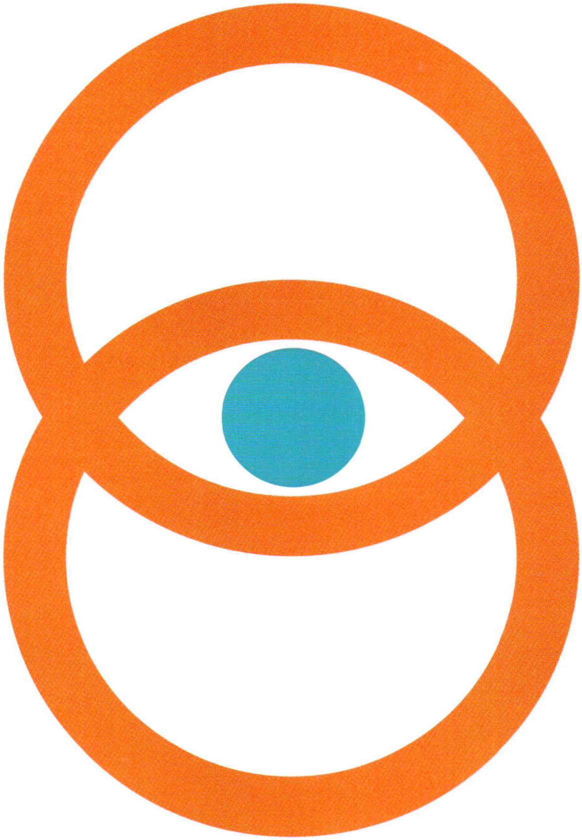

DIVINE FAITH / NON-ATTACHMENT

Divinely open to receive, I am wide to the notion that absolute faith requires a crystal clear non-attachment to beliefs which limit, to traits and self-inflicted restrictions which impose small and minded and thinking attempts at being full alive and in this minute, this now, this loving, dancing divinely faithful moment I am embraced, enraptured and enthused with the knowing that I can let go, stop my clinging to limits, labels, and the opinions of others.

There is one minute, I am in it. There is one guiding principle – Love and I am it. And we are One, divinely faith-full, completely and entirely available to heed the urging of the Divinest Plan . . . no rules, no commands, One request . . . believe, love, keep the faith and let go – Open your heart and hands and receive.

Thanks for the FAITH.
YOU Rock This Planet.

FAITH-FULLY wed to the DIVINITY I AM. I am filled with the seed of delivering speed to gallop along with the lifting passion of compassionate living and willing. I bet on infinity with my consistent walk to the center called my absolute spot, now delicious, ingenious and light. DIVINE FAITH is ripe in the tantalizing taste, elegant the space, the living grass, the swaying experience of knowing the value of absolute believing founded on the cornerstone of a rock most solid, your absolute FAITH in the DIVINITY called you. Without and within, all the same, all the one, all the other and the Other one. We proclaim the holy names, yours and mine, by the eternal flame, the arcing belief, the attendant relief that there's love in this house I call planet and home, and there's love in this temple I call happy embrace, held in the arms of the DIVINEST FAITH, my own God-embroidered, grace full embodiment of the heart of this moment. I am DIVINE. Let me recline within the arms of sweet surrender. God is lightly woven to become the fabric of this form I'm sharing in dancing tender within remember of the DIVINITY I AM. I am DIVINE in my resolute faith in the grand design. God is my light and my way, shining proof within the truth of DIVINE FAITH. I will align with the heart DIVINE. DIVINE FAITH.

THE DIVINEMENTS

KEY CODES 17 - 24

DIVINE WILL
DIVINE MIND
DIVINE DESERVING
DIVINE MOTIVATION
DIVINE ESTEEM
DIVINE STRENGTH
DIVINE LEARNING
DIVINE INTUITION

DIVINE WILL

I will stand firmly in the knowing embrace of the self that I AM. I am divinely led by the returning desire to that complete communion called loving surrender. I will bathe in the flooding yellow remembrance of magnetic desire pulling me home to the point of pulsing beacon calling for my sailing leap into the absolute middle of my own heart.

Life led by Divinity is life walked in peaceful surrender to the trusting understanding that you will walk and exactly the moment by unfolding moment that you are here to experience. Trust the ride, the adventurous delve into the realm of all possibility and infinite return on your willing investment.

WE WILL.

Will you surrender to the heart more tender, to the kindest render of a living remember? We are one and shining particles of the living son. Where is your heart now, where is her light? Fill her up at the loving cup, at the living light, at the splashing lip of a healing sip called DIVINE attention to the willing mention of the free-est mansion, the living passion of knowing the peace, the absolute bliss of the crystal clear design to align my living to the highest giving. The g's are gone. Gravity's felt my rekindle and I am slipping on boats of high resolution to picture this trip to the far side of bliss, circling round home to see that the light-in-the-middle is me, blinking soft within the realm of my kingdomed heaven, the crown I'm promised. The lotus I'm petaling is this heart-felt swelling to guide my willing return to the heart most fine and this light I call mine DIVINE to the ways of living my feel by the star swept band of my greatest fan. Hand in hand I dance to the spin of living my light by DIVINE WILL again. Know the son of the Buddha within. Light the night with your searing return to DIVINE WILL. Let the countdown begin.

Love is an inventive state
of energetic peace and a powerful release
to the rise apparent when God said
"Let there be Light" . . .
Humanity . . .

Enter now the halls of faith . . .
blessed be you and your BASIC HUMANITY.

DIVINE MIND

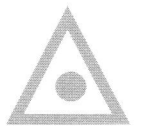

Clearing the space for Godly thinking is inclusive of clearing all blocking, knotty thoughtless patterns which by their fearing presence block and deny the return, the glorious tapping return to the crystal clear communication line, the gut truth, the Divine Mind. Your willing acceptance of our inherent ability to "tap in" to all knowing, all knowledge, is the key to learning divinely. We are the root, the trunk, and the branches of life's Tree of Knowledge. Trust your will and climb on out to the limitless limbs of the Divine Knowing, Learning, ALL SEEING MIND.

MIND-FULL to a moment, I feel DIVINITY swelling in the throat of my telling instinct to share the design and the plan of DIVINITY and I know that my telling is an infinite pillar of salty surrender to the humanity I AM and in this surrender I find a new ember, a milky wet moment of ambrosial content, a lightening exposure to the opportunity to hover near the edge of living plenty, to anchor in the feeling that earth spin's now revealing the floor beneath the ceiling, and standing on the reeling, I AM leaving tealing trails of blue-green resolute to sparkle in the healing flood of the life I call truth, and know me I'm knowing you and knowing us is proof that there's God here in the middle hills of my life-filled loving triangular approach to my angled, sacred, geometric scene called living mode and mean. You and me and God make three . . . body, MIND and spirit, let's hear the relief, the silent spring, of hearing your soft heart upon her own strings and the mind called the monkey, where's its old cap? Blown to the moon and to infinity beyond that Welcome the notion of celestial motion amid the spin of the DIVINITY I AM. I will align to DIVINE MIND.

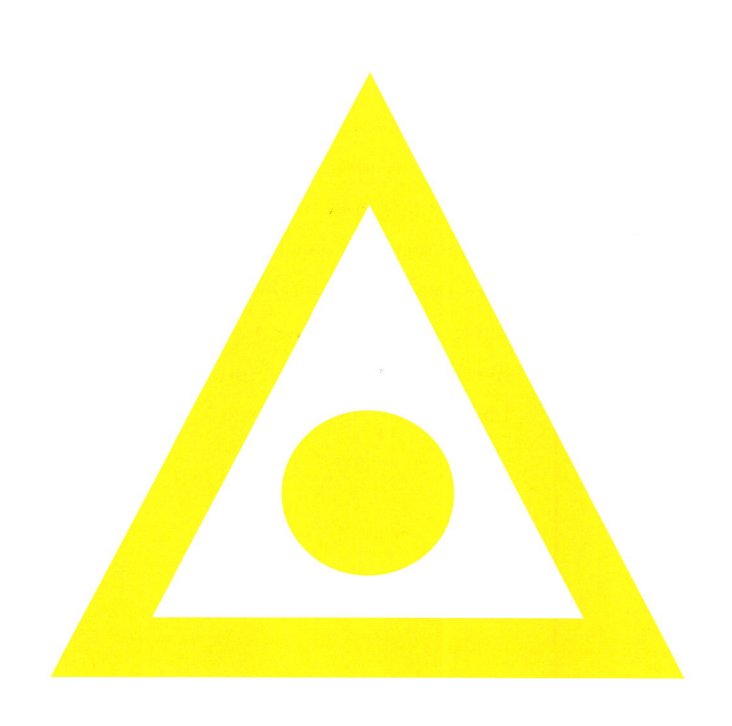

DIVINE DESERVING

When I know the expanse of our divine beauty, in that knowing moment I am struck with the lightning flash of realization that All is all that is acceptable for a part, a bulb of the One light. Examining my soul, I am given the options, the absolute creative role, the grand design, the astounding opportunity to remember my absolute inheritance as a daughter, as a son, as a spark of the One. I am arcing home to the explosive return of the knowing surrender to deserving to live Divinely, well, and full. I DESERVE in the Light of my Highest Desire.

DESERVING trails of infinite worth spiral within this planet called Earth. The Earth is a magnet for all who desire to live in the feeling of singing in choirs of Arc-angled giving and angelic retreat to the stars called the ceiling and the filling replete with sparkling wondering and happy magnetic. North to the border of a brand new planet. DIVINE to DESERVING I AM willing to lift my heart to a new level and my life to this trip-py reminder that flying takes balance and the living the "good" life requires a great talent, a knowing DESERVING, a living life-well, a telling revival of the happiness found by allowing forever to live in this town. And I AM going down, sweet seat, to rest this night in the glowing light of sweet surrender to DIVINE DESERVING.

DIVINE MOTIVATION

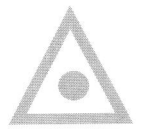

Living light pushes through the lethargy of my indecisive forgetting my missive, and I am filled with the releasing energy of a moment held spellbound, eternally moving and looping in dynamic, dancing, delightful designs of light, shimmering light dwelling full within the column of Absolute Knowing access to all that is and all that will be. I AM light in the Knowing I am divinely motivated to continue the creative dancing being of delight. Holy and Inspired.

I am MOTIVATED and DIVINELY sated by the invigorating news that DIVINITY is here and that I can rest in the views of latin content and spell out the truth that there is love in this tent, and the day and the night full-filled with the light constitute the proof that I AM living full sooth in the groove called DIVINE MOTIVATION. Himalayan heights echo invites to the table now fully set – let the banquet begin. Here comes Mother and friends to add a new plate and a message, it's late and DIVINELY I know that we are MOTIVATED homeward and onward and deeper inside by the cleft in the road which delivers our soul to the light of that proof. Know the facts, see the loop, feel the swell of my full-throated delivery. The World's recovery rests in the hands of our DIVINE MOTIVATION. Know your intentions, enjoy the invention, the humanity called you and the Basic humming news. The miracle is here, dancing rainbows clear across the waters. Earth's the altar, Father's meaning, Mother's leaning, catching you, inviting me to take a swim in our basic humanity by DIVINE MOTIVATION. Seeing you.

DIVINE ESTEEM

Divinely holding you sacred, I am held in the safest, warmest, lightest, ungrasping hands – my own, and I am light dancing and tossing and joyously arcing around and through and within the enormity of knowing just how delicious and delicate and resilient this wave that I am can be and is and I am ignited with Holy Fire and I am Absolutely and uniquely light and left free to swim light looping circles and splashing down in the center of my heart, I am held highest and well-deserved of knowing my Divinity esteemed.

Aloha.

Treva.

Welcome the seam which leads to the stream of the melting in the middle, the middle place, the hallowing ground, the basic sound of the welcoming near of the high-self ESTEEMED as I hear my own ear catching the loop, my lipping truth. Treva's home, insert your own name and ESTEEM it the same. Know the strength, the power of words met mingling with electric tingling filled with the tower, the column of light. Deep into night and oft through the day I am singing me home on an infinite way – seeing me, basically free, cleaning my hollow with the information gleaned. I am led to lift my head to the resting bed, a higher plane, a new understanding. I am standing well within the mind of living this time in the kindest entwine, this marker in space called an infinite mind. The body knows her resolute mind is in the center of living DIVINE and the portal's open and sacredly clear by the absolute release – Good-bye fear. I am home to rest my head in the infinite cradle of my high self, more able, to teach me the treat of walking this street, the road good and red, the middle yellowed leaning to the solar plexus leading. Know the mind, the body's kind try-angulation in this station of DIVINE ESTEEM. ESTEEMING ME. I am led to see our basic DIVINITY. Shining still within the middle. Run the symbol magnetic clearing. Past-times fleeing. Love is clearing all the corners to sweep this forgetting web to the border of forgiving order. I AM home and led to the land of DIVINE ESTEEM. A natural selection.

DIVINE STRENGTH

Divinity inherently has the integrity of a knowing showing absolute space of shared electrical intensity clearing the blocking forgotten webbing I am reminded of the integrity of knowing my divine backbone, my towering sparkling power. I AM absolute. I AM known and the knowing. I am held as Absolute and well strengthened by the knowing light shining forth through my believing heart. Ah men – Know thy strength held tight in the light of one moment's glowing showing.

Darwinian keening and Popal Vuh teaching, and miraculous seeing of the immaculate conception that all is the One and the same in the sun of our natural selection to feel the tower of the riveting reception, the consistent reflection of the intimate direction to know thyself and be free. Look at me reflecting you and your Basic Humanity, in my penning truth fishing for men upon the shores of your feminine land. Attention given in love received within the sleeves of my loving arms. God has charms called you and me, infinity's tree, the creative belief that loves knows the freedom and remembers the night of a delicate sight. Arcing home I am led to live alone within the spread of my wide expanse, my templed treat, the love I AM, the lighted belief that there's DIVINITY here. There lies my STRENGTH. For in knowing you, I am knowing me, and that is Basic Humanity. DIVINELY seen, there's power in the blood coursing full to my veins, full with DIVINITY's own. Seeking home, I am led to the pool within and I know the baptism of a living fire, my resting swim in the living fountain and the DIVINE STRENGTH to see the DIVINITY I AM. God is real – just take a feel of my lifted hand. Who's the man? We are STRENGTH by design. DIVINE STRENGTH.

DIVINE LEARNING

I AM learning that all knowing is divinely held, lightly remembered by my sparking, arcing, return to the point of all remembering and when I'm held from knowing alas my slip is showing and forgotten is my success to the one who knows All best and I am held in wonder at the thundering pleasing returning sound of my heart's beating remembering of the forevering that is applauding my DIVINE Returning to Knowing.

The intimate glance at the welcome chance to remember just all that I am and technologically speaking I want the experience of operating in every sense, in every way, within the sway of the botanical stay, the environmental play of the hallelujah day, what pray, shall we do? Play at the being, at the intricate weaving of becoming the seeing, the wellness in the treeing, the mushrooming eyesight called seeing the opening, invoking the feeling, embracing the ceiling, escaping the third slot directed by far, to shift to the Gemini twin on the floor of the other, the fire side elliptic, the spirit side opening, the embrace of clouds – lightly I'm woven and gently I'm flowing in the cell-a-brating swing of another heart's singing, lifting to the joy that I am gifting you, straight through the middle, and light I am singing with DIVINE leaning into the LEARNING. I AM curving back home to me and free. LIGHT DIVINE guide by sweet heart's returning to DIVINE LEARNING. Cell by Cell. The teacher . . . the student. The friend.
All is well within my DIVINE LEARNING.

DIVINE INTUITION / GUT

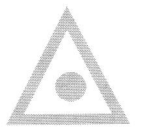

Showing in the approaching is the divining rod of gut-tuition showing me the light bouncing back as full or less. If full, the path is open. If lessened then I am knowing that the loop of possibility is allowing a lobbing return of my tennis balled heart's shot off the top of the net. Re-examination and heightening of my gut's ability to carry lighter tension creates shots which float gently over the top and the racquet stops and a bell rings crystal – well done – Divine Intuition speaking —
Carry On . . .

DIVINE yearning is the guiding light, the gut wide teacher, the return of the light winged giving, this optimum living. I am well within the grip of my dancing hips and swollen tipped drinking of the gifted singing called hearts are ringing. Welcome swell of the infinite knowing that DIVINITY is showing in my return to the light inside. I AM feeling. In all ways healing. My decadent fix is the living this rich, testing growing all ways flowing by DIVINITY led and by my heart well read. I am the light and the leading lip of a waving return to trusting your yearning as a needle pointing the way to your issue for the day. Lead the night into the LIGHT of a brand new beginning to precious initiating return to my DIVINE anticipation of the living spin, view then the lines of DIVINE design. I am led to recline in color toned retreat at the love-driven controls of my DIVINE INTUITION.

THE DIVINEMENTS

KEY CODES 25 - 32

DIVINE LOVE
DIVINE PEACE
DIVINE COMPASSION
DIVINE SHARING
DIVINE HARMONY
DIVINE O - MISSION
DIVINE DELIGHT
DIVINE REST

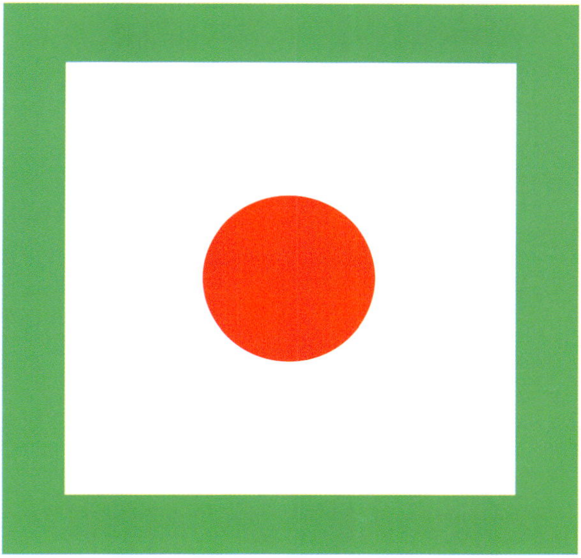

DIVINE LOVE

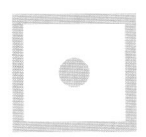

Arcing home to the heart of delighted infinity, I am free, energized and ecstatically exuberant in the sharing return, the sparkling intensity of this continued prosperity to remember that essentially we are LOVE, we are shared sparks of the Sharing One Source generating full through the breathing heart of the Sun's sparkling return to the heart of her being – Sparkling gently, breathing light, lightly shining in the divining experience of a personal relationship with the Source of our Source. To the light – loving on – the light's on.

A greater LOVE hath man and yet how often we forget that the peace of the sister is mother of the brother and I am led to lift high my head to listen, heart well and content and effervescently lit with ecstatic release at the lip of a breeze to the light of DIVINITY's lofty tale. DIVINER LOVE hath man than this, and knowing bliss is remembering light and I am wide to a dream and breath to breath. I am met by an essence, my own, shimmering home on wave after wave of lilting season, bliss by bliss in leafy return to the infinity I've yearned to enkindle with my level-handed shake of the equivalence called forever's Eden, and in the paradise of corona's dancing rhyme, know the rhyme of the Earth's balance and the equality of her spin and the equilibrium of her giving, and I am swept to shatter the walling. I'm willing to simpering, swelling, umbilical return to the silver-corded release, the laughing attendance to the welling intrigue, not my sleeve, ever my heart, I am led by . . . the living spark . . . the many dressed, often tested, never wasted return to remembering the heart, my own and calling her by name, his lilting refrain. DIVINE LOVE.

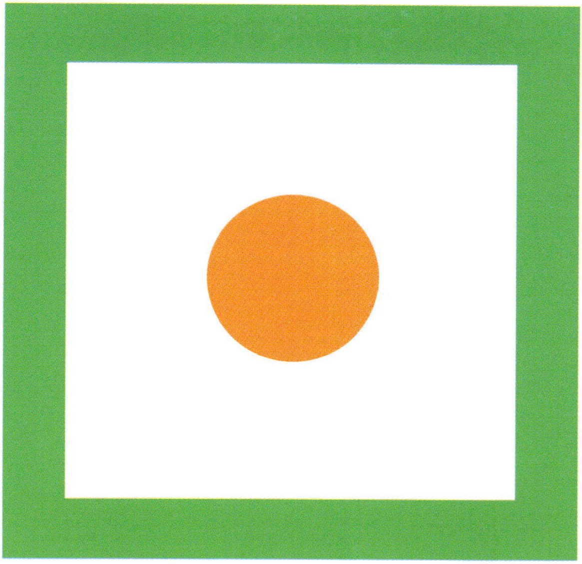

DIVINE PEACE

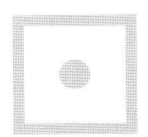

Peacefully pleased with the promise of potent, pressing, penitent releasing – I am floating free – Bouncing heart to heart, spark to spark, melting breathing and walled-in forgetting. Letting me in, breathing with me, we remember our knowing, swimming, cruising, surfing excitement, light riding light, carrying light, sharing light, we are led to the point of all creation, to the place of breathing love, lovingly led to the position of receiving, the peaceful, pleasing return to the place of a full heart.

PEACEFULLY bright I am led to the light of remembering elegance akin to my blissing loft to surrender within to the life giving blend called life which is swell and soft and melting tonight in the lapping band, caribbean and blue and gentle. I AM the Ocean of Life and 78% emotive and motile slim, I slide into the thrill of pleasant appraisal and recognizant attraction to the bridge of beaming, believing, and elegantly slim-sided with yellow-green grains of tiny membraned mitochondia tastes of angelic singing, thrilling and telling, spiritually speaking. Tibetan ringing is feeling the ceiling of a Chinese revealing, know the truth, the proof in you, the farthest view is DIVINITY'S hue. A rainbow's explosion of a commune's erosion. The love is true, the peace is free and the Tibetan in me says that the Chinese review requires the full invocation of the law of One and the land of the setting sun has begun. Know the peace of knowing me as you and we are free in our knowledgeable release to DIVINE peace. The middle East. Know release. The light is on. Know the sun. The son is home. The prayer wheels spun. Embrace the tree beneath which we sit in peace-full surrender to the Enlightenment of knowing our DIVINE PEACE. Know your heart and your kneeling taste of the Buddha's face and the delicate spin of living within the mountainous return to the lake of all One. DIVINE PEACE.

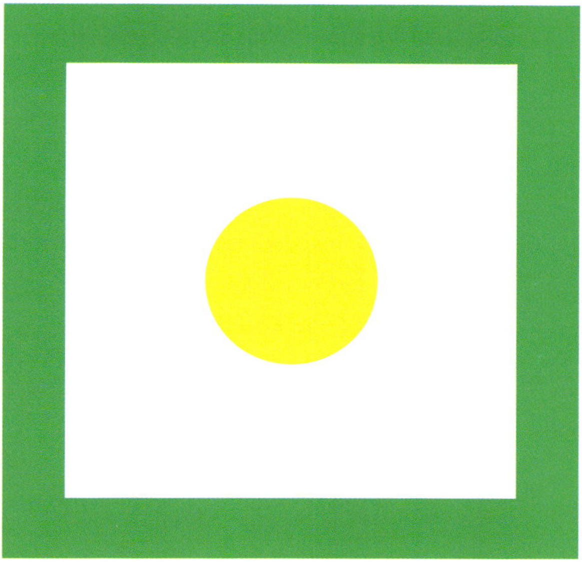

DIVINE COMPASSION

Baby, tiny innocent, you show me, in my face
peering lovingly into yours that eye-to-eye
we are held divine and passion surges through
me for I am compassioned with the absolute
return to the absolute reminder of who I am,
who I am, who we are – on the inside where
it counts – growing, filling, remembered C-elf *
is swelling full within the walls of cells reminded
that home and hearth and living in the center
brings loving surrender, tender forgiving and
impassioned compassion for the mirrored
reminders of whom we are – simply divine
for-giving, and compassioned.

* *The cellular self*

COME-PASSION, I call, COMPASSION I AM.
The tree of the life and the love of a man. DIVINE from the start and welcome to see the visionary excellence of our awakening DIVINITY. Know the peace of our living nirvanic return to the kingdom within. The kingdom rings with freedom's peal and I know the wheel of release to the truth that we are land and the living peace. Know the proof. The light in you warms my heart with the beauty of knowing that your DIVINITY is showing in your COMPASSIONATE glowing. I am the moon and the sun and the stars and your dancing infusion of the passion of Mars. The healing is here and the people need see the absolute loving of my heart's infinity. All-ways I lead and All-ways I pray for the healing return of the holiest face. Know your own reflecting near in the crystal eyes of those held dear. Live the proof. Walk the faith. Share what's said in kneeling inclusion of our loving embrace of the infinite tread, the blending revival at the living edge of this nation's ledge to uphold integrity and truth and the waving grains of our presidential gains met by the life lived integral and replete with welcome excitement and pleasure that loving is the treasure to be held like the Magna and Carta, the *Qwan and the Yin, of the COMPASSIONATE return to the home my own. And I am led by design to the corner of the street called COMPASSIONATE DIVINITY. Let it be. DIVINE. ME. COMPASSION . . . for my self and your hear too. Sister friendly I remain by my caring refrain, your name, DIVINE COMPASSION.

*The Chinese Goddess of Compassion

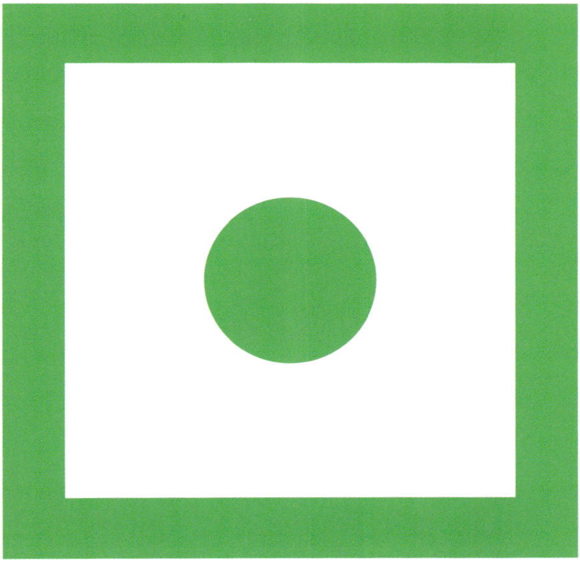

DIVINE SHARING

Share this with your neighboring hearts – we are light bouncing balls of unlimited potential . . . All that is available is absolutely available as long as I believe and know that there is plenty to give and plenty to share. I remember that sharing includes receiving on my part and on your behalf. I graciously agree to accept your often timid, sometimes raging attempts at bridging the gap and I am led and I swell with the flowing, encouraging potential of knowing that the greater my capacity for living is known, the greater the living is the giving light of sharing the shedding of limited being. Share the joyous knowing of – DIVINE LUMINOSITY SHARED.

DIVINITY'S SHARING her gentle caring, her delicate weave of my knowing being and I am defined by the well-fed lines of giving caring which trace my design. I am the find and the found and the bound for glory. Know this well and exhale in living fill of the delicate thrill of finding recline in the hammock of life's greatest SHARING. Our light is carrying the news to the delicate, the dull, and the slightly obtuse. Angled to receive and destined to give, I am wearing it well and living to give. DIVINITY'S SHARING in my giving caring and I am wearing the news in designer shoes and watching my tracks – you can see that I'm back to living light well and feeding the mass I call me – with a lifetime supply of basic DIVINITY. Basically Human and eternally DIVINE, I resign to the refrain of the holiest name, my own, sweet refrain. Let us remain ecstatic and well in our living giving of the light I AM living, by my DIVINE SHARING.

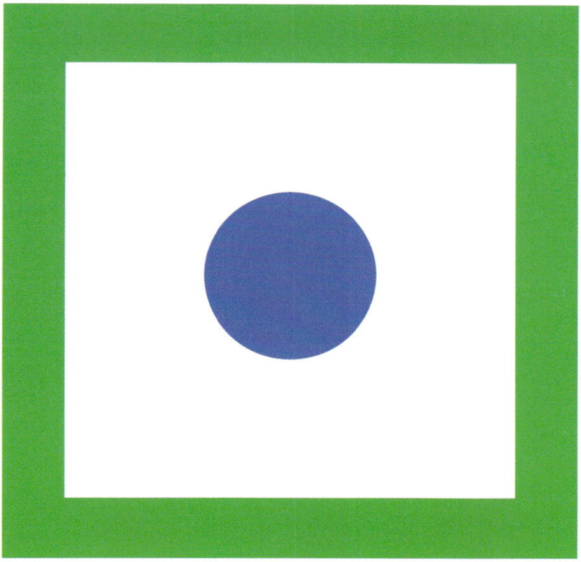

DIVINE HARMONY

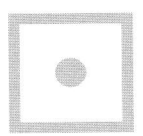

Harmony is arcing through your Be-ing Inspiring you to dance your way – gentle – into creation's flowing sway. Feel the pulling, embracing opening of peaceful surrender to your divine nature. We are nature's divine light seeking Absolute Harmony. Harmony is beckoning your spiraling continuation of the convergent resurgence of energy reconnecting to the beckoning, filling peaceful abundance of knowing living swelling return. We are peace, blissing our harmonious dancing return to the well of All living to the centering heart of all being – our own – and in this dance we respond to the remembrance of harmonious delight.

Sing me a song and bring this along, harmony's tree, the freeing ability to soar dear in flight to the feathery shore of a trilling night's dream and awake to the slam I AM inclined to align to the magic within, my celestial friend. Life's kindest notion is the silence of devotion balancing free in spinning eternity. Nature's in this balance and the total is sweet. It's the integrity of your tap dancing feet lighting the way by eternity's flame, and nearing the curve and the point of this rhyme, welcome yourself to the living this time, marching homeward on octaves ecstatic to know the full truth of the life led dramatic and easy and sweet, and the feel of your loving, breathing feet leading the pack, the choir, that All, to the celestial orb, the mighty Earth ball, and the law of ALL ONE returns on the line and I am now dancing to 3.14, echoing tunes illuminating the floor with ecstatic design and patterns with flair, and the exuberant light woven dancing. Mid-air on the curve of a wave I am lightly held eternally living life's harmonic swell. Nature seeking balance. Homeward leads the chalice. Spilling hints of glacial melt, filling streams with eternal lift and ringing on the firmament's lip, know a man, count the sands, trip the span of living light well. Life's DIVINE spin. The echotic tale. The man symphonic. DIVINE HARMONY. Pi to the sky and all the way through. The symphony of you. The lightest refrain. The living song of getting along . . . All One. Sung in DIVINE HARMONY. Light DIVINE.

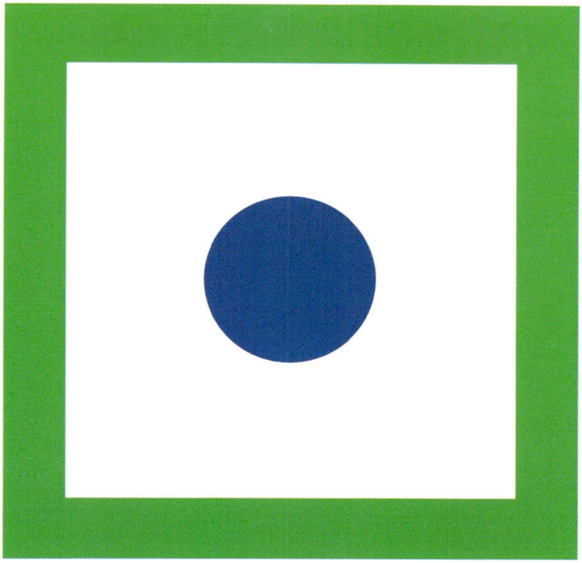

DIVINE O-MISSION (MAKING SPACE)

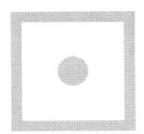

Within the gaps of landings between flights,
I remember the mission and my commission to
embrace the void, the opening, the space, and I
am connected again and sailing into the space of
divine flighted, dancing, aborted crashing into
the ground of senseless forgetting. I am lifted
home and light arcing home, heart-to-heart,
burning red and green stripes of melting loving
acceptance swell green and pink, and dripping
red delighted splashes flow gently into the space
created by my knowing allowance of the beauty
of diving off the edge – trusting my trusting
nature, space is created by O - Mission.

DIVINELY aware of this infinity we share I welcome the void and the line and the rhyme and the eloquent review of this particular hue, rainbowed and blue to a moonstone's review, I am welcome to see the divinity's true height, light, and I am level and read . . . by the hand that said, that these commands and let them be fed to the knowing truth that energetically there's proof that honoring my father and mother makes me wise and well to eternity. See this spatial increase of the facial truth that resting is swell and diving is well in my adult O-MISSION of other's entangles. Hear, know the story. There, know this proof. The theorem called evil has gone to the light, and DIVINITY'S calling to reveal the news . . . there's always been only one way. The Living Truth. You and Me. Eternity's Tree. Of this Life let me say, I AM definitely led to see the creation in your light affinity. Know the light by DIVINE O-MISSION. Know your position. Creation's waiting to see the life burning soft in your eyes tonight. Love's aloft in the taste for a delicate space, light by DIVINE O-MISSION. Know your purpose. LIGHT.

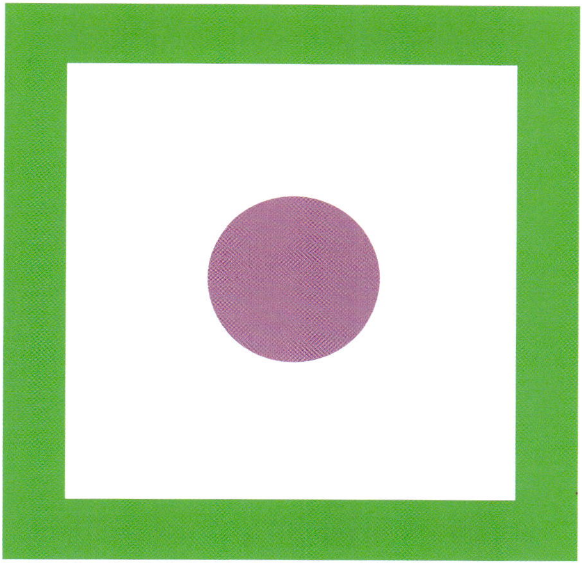

DIVINE DELIGHT

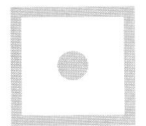

Welcome your heart to the Part resounding swelling, splashing in the center of your passionate, peaceful, loving embracing heart – you are well, you are well-loved, you are embraced in delightful dancing surrender – share the light, share – de-vinity, share abundance of being be-lighted, be-knighted, be mesmerized with your attention to the delight-full look on each other's heart, and face, and soul full of love lift your happy heart to the light and remember delight of the dancing, swirling, shimmering, arcing light being which you embody.
Welcome to the light.
You are my delight.

Metatron

DELIGHT-FULLY led, the surface I sea, and the waves splashing warm are the beauty in me, and my life is led by a delicate tread on an infinite curl and an elegance said too often to be forgotten . . . Light by all rights, light, let it be, the infinite security of living my life free. Now I tread, softly led by a delicate proof, inside I am truth, full and fed by the pulsing red burst of this morning's passion-ate return to the land of ALL remember. I am the cinder and the lava and the red return of the prodigal me to the eyes, yours and mine, we are fine within the tread of our delicacy fed to believe that now comes reprieve – know the taste of an intellectual eclectic rain dance brought to bring our be-ing to springy revival past the web of survival, our climbing return to the fantastic land, the living revival of well beyond survival. We are loving this land and we are grand and balanced to blend within the ecstasy of our living surrender. Love here is healthy. Hear and know the DIVINITY of me delicately seamed to the One light, ours, and eternally grand in my giving insight to the DIVINE DELIGHT, I AM.

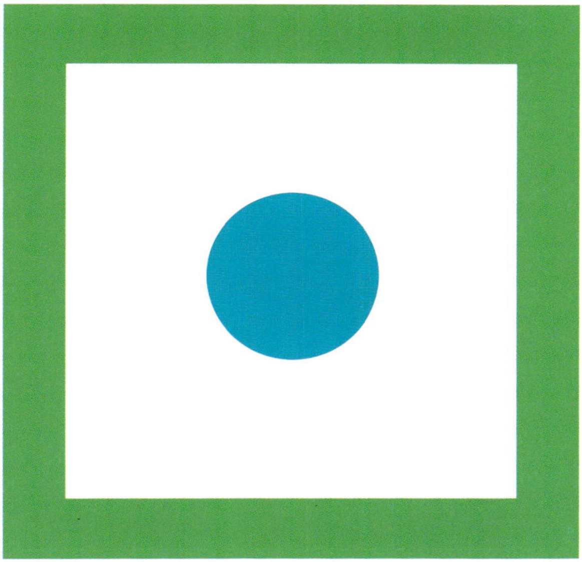

DIVINE REST / SPLASH DOWN

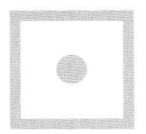

Chilling out, hanging loose, splashing down in the center of the Ah Ha remembrance of who I AM, we are welcomed to the rest of the seventh day of creation. You are your own creation and Now we Know it. Let us move gently forward to the embracing surrender to the flowing light filling the center of our being sharing. Rest awhile in the heart of us. I love you my dearest light being. Thank you for the notion of swimming in the ocean of All light's droplets sparkling in the light of the Light's embracing bosom. AND ON THE SEVENTH DAY WE RESTED.

Blessed in my be-ing there is delicate receiving and
DIVINE discretion at the living direction I AM led to Be-lieve
and knowing the Mother I AM, the recovery of an elegant seed is
solid and satin in my leathery palm, and I AM emotive and well
and delivering the tale that you are DIVINE and I AM fine, and
lacey I swing in life's arcing recall that I AM the love sailing free in
the space and the span and the rainbow tree stretching between the
Earth and Sky and Grandmother's singing and little sister's sung.
The whales of remember spout great gulps of grand design for the
whales know the seaming, they remember the trail of the stars circling heaven and their coming to see the Earth and the Heaven in
the DIVINITY called me, and I am dreaming in great numbers and
I am living to tell the elevated practice of living love's swell.
I am DIVINITY'S light vocation and I am here to say, let it be,
me, the Living tree. The symbol and the span and the land of the
free. The span, mighty, unsealed and clean and living soul-free.
I AM DIVINE, toe to head, and as it's said . . . Let us test the lap
of receiving. God made us man, and man, we made God in our
breathing rememberance to surrender to DIVINE REST.
The best and the rest. DIVINELY HU-MAN.

THE DIVINEMENTS

KEY CODES 33 - 40

DIVINE COMMUNICATION
DIVINE REVEALING
DIVINE LISTENING
DIVINELY SPEAKING
DIVINELY WORDS FOR-GIVING
DIVINELY WORDS FOR-LIVING
DIVINELY PRAISES RINGING
DIVINE DESIGN

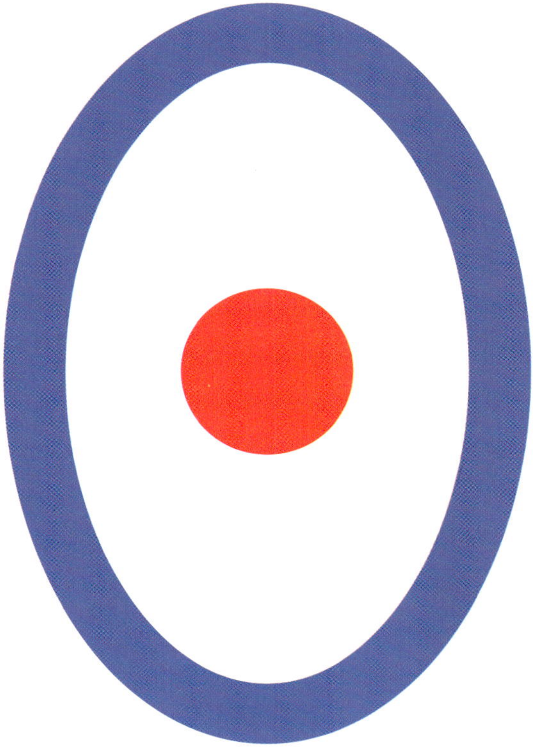

DIVINE COMMUNICATION

Ask for the divinity to speak with the crystal clear voice of an oracle singing sweet communication of light participation through the knowing opening in the center of your beyond thinking surrender to singing – communicating beyond words, without the desire to enforce your surrender to hearing the gentle droplets, the trickles, the crystalline quality of the gems of my engendered, spirit - tendered appreciation of the love and the light and the beginning which you are for me, in me, through me. Join me in singing in unison and in delight; you are the One and in that knowing my heart is showing my glowing remembrance of our DIVINE COMMUNICATION.

Unlock the lessons and make a New Deal. The tower resolute is a column near here and here are the pencils, the trees and the branch. Write what you feel and take a great chance, a stand, and deliver an increase of zeal. We are the kindest, the reverend, the light-headed interpreters of living this life. Your hear knows the impress, the ingress, the rhyme – just ask us again, we are living life fine to the middle and central coaxial and digital by facsimile. I'm smiling at someone who's looking like me. Set it free. It's basic, the message, the spinning infinity, the tree called resurrection is trilling with forgiving news. Know the glow of freeing your flow. Tell the man about the span, I AM, and know the bliss of the blending Kiss, the whistling release of the minimal-less existance for the elequent bliss of telling it "like it is" for you. True COMMUNICATION knows the beauty of living well and loving example and breathing arrival of the latest truth the living proof. You are alive and well and grown to tell that peace is a rainbow and grace is a knowing that your infinity is showing in your desire to express oblivious stares at the love and the light. I AM shining Arcturial through the night and delighted by the flight. Home to say – DIVINELY on time. DIVINE COMMUNICATION.

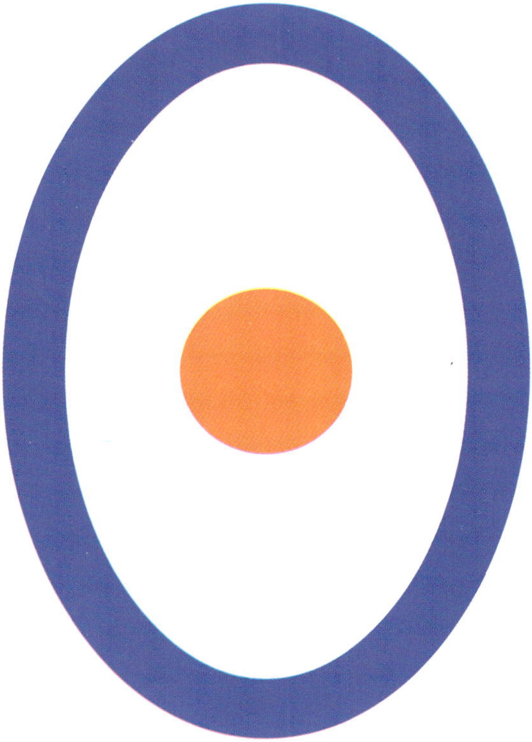

DIVINE REVELATION

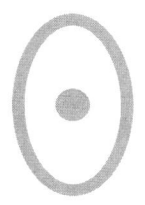

My words are revealing the crystal clear
quality of the intentional import of light speaking
through me, in me, arcing fondly to the ears of
your feet, the eyes of your head, the belly button
breathing in the navel of your deepening return
to the edge of your world. Paint the edges with
light brushes, light melting edges of gentle
communication open my heart and I see the
expanse, I hear the beyond dimension singing
of your tourmalined winging revelation, of
amplified, electrical conviction. You are the
Divine revelation, the beginning and the Alpha
– the inspiration and the arc initiating contact
with the source of All beginning beaming being –
Aloha Abha* – my beloved.

*Abha - The center of the heart for all people on earth.
Where the heart and breath meet.*

I am REVEALING the telling truth. I AM a prophet and a sage. You too know the feeling of DIVINITY REVEALING in your standing address, that there's love in this test of total accept and absolute give. Deliver the sender full address to know the best and the greatest rest in the arms of a cradling forever. I AM, and I am given the right to fight the discover that leads like no other to the edge of the day and the lip of the night, full in flight, led to sight along the arm of a loving whaling vision . . . the Earth is given the right to elevate your sight on the brightest star and the orangest bar of frozen delight. The moon is full and Mars is living in giving surrender to the living blender. You, my celestial cocktail of an ambrosial mix, your DIVINITY sticks to the point. I love you and you are DIVINE in your REVEALING truth. Know the proof. LIGHT by DIVINE REVELATION. ME. YOU. LIGHT.

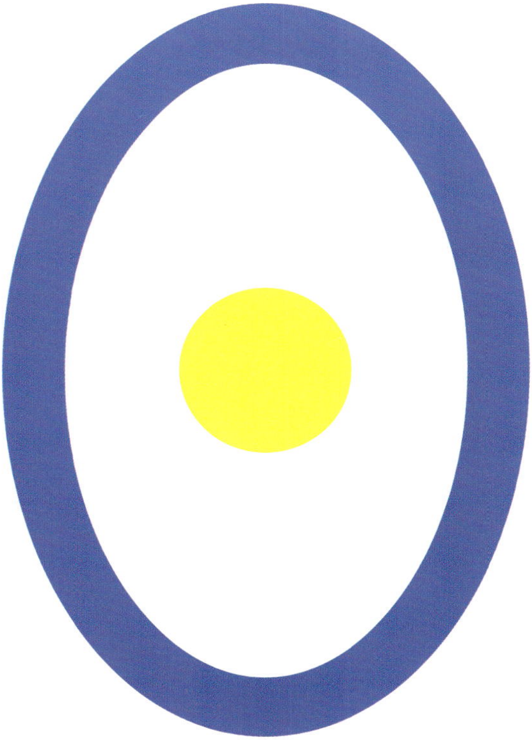

DIVINE LISTENING

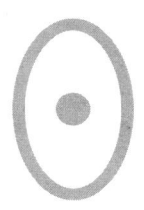

Listen to this – your heart is speaking
passionate wellings of holy impassioned winging.
This ringing is true – the listener is you –
melt away the showing, the lines are open
and your face is beaming your heart's delightful
message. Transmissions of rosey quartz quality
explode pink and wet and rich in a kinetic rush,
and without speaking, I listen to the silent
meaning of your ears ringing – Honest replies are
one of life's most loving gifts, and still silent
I fall gently into the eyes of ONE Knowing
golden DIVINE LISTENING.

Are you LISTENING, and were you well in your reeling delivery of the love that tells no more stories and knows more the lies? I see revealing shining full in your eyes and lifting my divisions I know that we are One and in my lawing living I understand the truth, my mottos known throughout this land. You are the infinite loop. Deliver now your living house, your loving DIVINE stars of pink and green reminder that the revelation says the seals and horses and lions and lambs can live the surrender to the star, I AM. Know the mind. the God of time-ing extraction and definite action, that's you and me and DIVINITY'S free flowing sign, infinity's time to a T. Tell the truth. Know the proof. You are DIVINE in your LISTENING kindness and your elegant fine-tuned reception of my DIVINE VOICE. Live the choice, LIGHT. By DIVINELY spoken LISTENING, recline. DIVINE LISTENING.

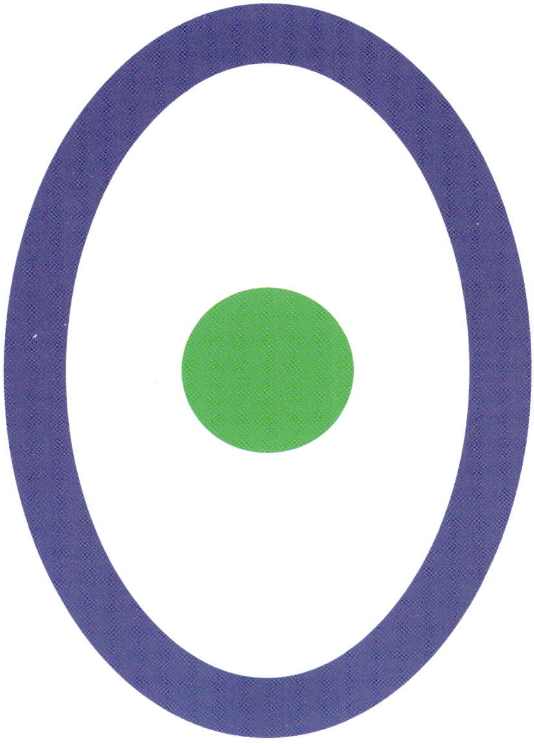

DIVINE SPEAKING

Droplets voice their anticipation of the emancipation, the power of speaking truly what loving yourself fully and completely and wholly sounds like. The full immersion is the key to noting your given ability to embrace the vocalization of expectancy, of expression of the swelling creative tendency which fills the well and empties the heart and makes room for the next breathing filling of the loving thrilling return of all possibility, all delight, delicious delight-full infinite singing sounds belling clear and ringing out the news – We are DIVINE. Fill your voice, feel your light . . .
DIVINELY SPEAKING.

SPEAK this truth. We are proof that living right means living LIGHT and living light means willing rightfull expression of your giving discretion to the word, now SPOKEN. I am devoted to the knowing that your DIVINITY is showing in your absolute bliss at the brink of a kiss lifting Light to a new bliss by design DIVINE, telling difference this time. We are so fine and so well defined in our singing revealing of the lift to right. Rhyming scheming has led to singing restitution of our contemporary landscaped tale – know the swell of living well within the seams of a winding scheme. Schematically struct I am the tower of standing delivery here at the edge of my infinity – loop to loop. All the scoop. DIVINELY SPEAKING.

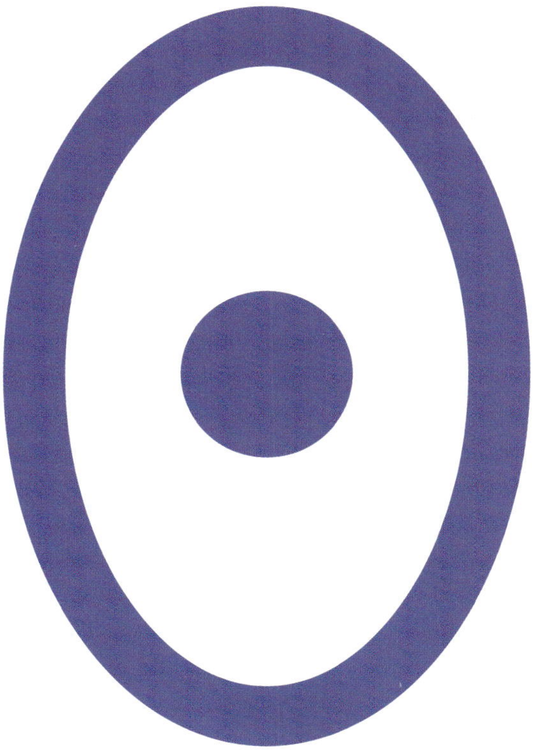

DIVINE WORDS FOR-GIVING

Tonight I spent the night on buying vowels
to right the feeling left when thinking flooded
wording bursts through dancing knowing and
I am left with showing active loving in my
divinely worded giving. You are my light-full
reason for both giving and receiving and in this
communication I see the Way and Truth and
Speaking clearly seeing is the way to keep
believing, and believing becomes knowing and
knowing truth is ringing and keeps this soul full
singing in arcs of divinely worded giving.
Well Spoken.

FOR-GIVEN, there's the key. FOR-GIVENESS, as for me, and in my house . . . Light or the subject. FOR-GIVENESS – that's right and only right by energetic law of the integral aspect of the Absolute One. All of us word-by-word FOR-GIVING proof that DIVINITY's truth is light attraction, a whirling action and a welcome sight. Light by design, a telling time and DIVINELY WORDS FOR-GIVING ring my tongue with crystallized content, intentionally sent, I AM the line of living fine. By design, and DIVINELY WORDS FOR-GIVING line my lip in an elequent kiss, a lightening touch, a tender much,in my DIVINELY WORDED FOR-GIVING. Light to the point, DIVINITY speaks to us . . . THE FOR-GIVING WORD. LIGHT. DIVINELY SPOKEN.

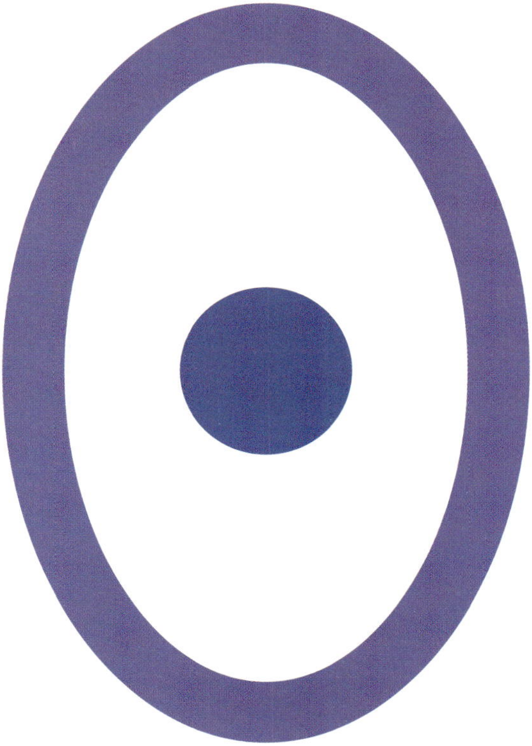

DIVINE WORDED LIVING

Singing and walking the talk that I'm talking is the secret to speaking my actively divinely worded living. Talking plus walking equals peace flooding compassionately in trickling aquamarine nuggets of light filled knowing. Show me your living example of spoken compassion, of forgiving, of singing, ringing blissfull light and I'll show you my lilting divinity in my every spoken step. You are the light shining bright in the place where words share the walk. Lead us on.

Sing us home . . .
Verb to heart . . .
Foot to ear . . .
DIVINELY.
WORDED.
LIVING.

DIVINITY'S LIVING for giving and in me that's enough to wake me up and to say, the giving's light and the seeing's fine and roaring is thunderous and the Be-ing kind and I have arranged to see the design of an infinite beauty of Hu-man design. An entering breath, an audible flow, a penetrating essence of the giving show. Today and tonight I AM at the delivery called Be-ing tender. Trickling trinkets of trivy-less joy and spinning up on humming wings, I know the employ of LIVING life well and fed and embraced by the dancing tread of your smiling face chanting me on to the brink and the sun of a rising horizon, the ascension has come, arising eastward and giving us goals to see the Sun's advice now of a living light. One song to the center and eternally I AM sung to the tune of the rain's drop and the purple-green breeze of lemon-aid lands and tangerine trees bringing me home on electric span. Hallelujah has risen from the lip of a LIVING light. See the WORD, DIVINELY heard. DIVINELY WORDS FOR LIVING. I AM. WE ARE. ALL ONE. Let it be. DIVINITY.

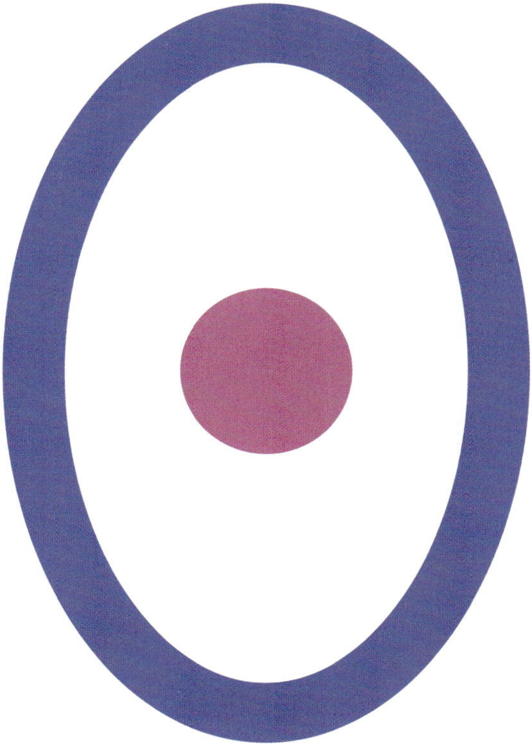

DIVINE PRAISES RINGING

Liberty sings of the resonance accepting our
round voiced peeling heavenward and homeward
we arc to the light singing forth between the
windows looking in. Spirit's speaking in praises
ringing, in divinely worded, humming, sounding,
pleasing, peeling, a light is shining in the petals
pearling open, gifted praising. Hallelujah we are
risen. Crosses offered. Conviction proffered.
Praises ringing. Burdens lifted – here's the
gifting – you are whole, you are divine,
you are the notes on the staff of one's praising
ringing. Oh sweet resurrecting light – Sing On.

Drums are chanting, strums are stringing, delicate facets are mathematically singing the pi'ing return of a living bird – the beak of the truth and a beaker of love, a life held full gentle in a giving flood of tympanic leaning and galactic keening. The kestrel has flown and she is welcome home to taste the space called sacred and well. Know the expanse of living this time. Enter in to the holiest shrine – your loving self – sacred, DIVINE, and elevated living with a pent-house view. Feel the confines pass in a flash of recognizant viewing and ecstatic splash. You are free by design. Know the peace of the lasting place of the Lords of the pi. 3.14 and a hole lot more, squared by design to energize the scene that Einsteinan notion and quantum motion declared unique, and wait till we see the Light full tympanic RINGING in me – DIVINELY singing, voices RINGING the eloquent news that DIVINITY is me and you too. Bend your knees to see the view, the humble seat, the sweetest slice of an infinite pie. ME. Eternally Infinite. DIVINELY let them sing the news, the holy praise – our heaven phase – LIGHT by DIVINE design. A heavenly composer – Me. Hear it sung. You. The Living proof and sweet we sing. LIGHT.

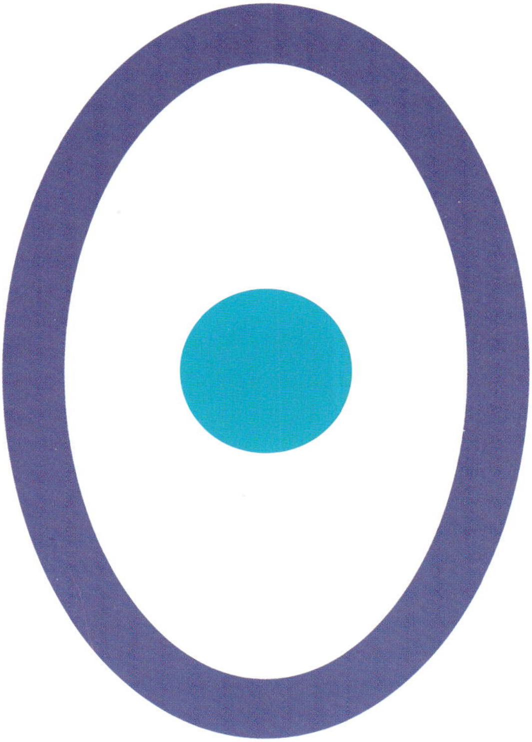

DIVINE DESIGN

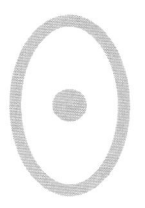

There is a line, a threaded knowing, which
lives in the showing example of how it's all
flowing – enter knowing, enter living, enter
giving the credit where due (that's to you)
and to me I'll be living sewing shut forgotten
stitching of the fabric of forgetting for the veil is
open, gaping, glad in showing this quilt we are
making of blocks of light touching squarely at the
edges painted fairly soft, gently shining, even
blurring – we are One-ing in the sunning return
to the patchwork knotting us all smoothly fitted
in this puzzle we call light.

Sacredly stated, we are the line and the rhyme, the reason the square of the pentagons drawin to a circling stare at the points of surrender in the life of a fair maiden, a welcome pagan, a nodding laden with knowing the pause and the pace and the fit of a laughing reminder that this is the slip and the centering tread. Dance to revival and sing in the choir of circling the square in the center of your eyes, stretched to thin – disguise – I am illuminated here by my giving stare directly into the LIGHT. I AM. Sacredly geometric now is the sine of the meaning more golden, the love on the line arcing cotangent to the bridge of the mind and lifting the miracle of loving incline. Enjoy the tribute, to the art of the square, circling in wrinkles of suring mid-air to the middle and gentle we thin the appraising revival of the delicate lift. This is my temple, my living gift and these are my eyes by vesica piscean pairs of pleadian agenda eliminating stares entreaty – filled to remember this sign, that life in the center is the surrender of flight's now forgotten by archaic align and the light full electric is on by advent of the 7-day beauty that loving has sent, and I am eternal and brilliantly bent to the lifetime of spinning DESIGN to lift high the banner of finishing lines of waiting acceptance and glittering stare at the heart of the tender, eliptic flare . . . illuminating skies and the heavens inside with the magnificent three returning to ride the elevated pair to the moon advantageous – and then eternity's stare at the lasting pear, know the taste of a luscious debate, we are free by DIVINE DESIGN, to live in the tree that's lightly me. DIVINE to a line and living fine in the branches eternal, the LIGHT in the sky, the leaves called your eyes. Keep them clear by DIVINE DESIGN and LIGHT perusal of the temple's internal care, your fair share. LIGHT, by DESIGN.

THE DIVINEMENTS

KEY CODES 41 - 48

DIVINE LIGHT
DIVINE KNOWING
DIVINE BROW-SING
DIVINE ATTENTION
DIVINE INTENTION
DIVINE INTEGRATION
DIVINE I AM
DIVINE MEDITATION

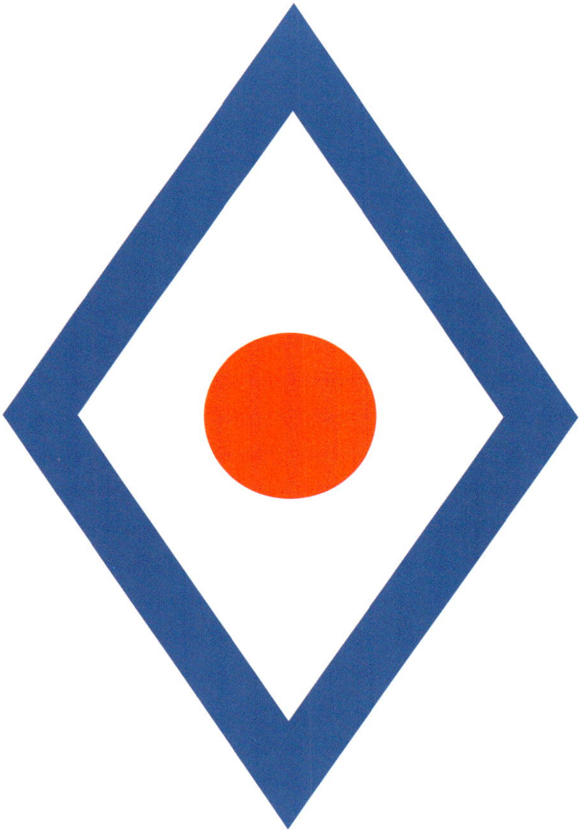

DIVINE LIGHT

The Light Is On. Welcome Home.

DIVINE this proof, this sacred theory, this emphatic blend of listening wattage, and know I this trend, this waking dream illuminated free by my absolute refusal to be less than thee. For I know the living God and the ENLIGHTENED man and the bridging span, the rainbow's grace and the living news that being LIGHT brings. Being LIGHT – now there's some news. Express it well from your elevated shoes. We are the holy ground, the holy span, the covenant lives in everyman. Raise your hand to electric swell, the loving space, the living well of fountainic splendor and splashing retreat. There's news at the end of this electric street, and it's you and the blues have attained a violet hue and a periwinkle dream. The LIGHT is on. A schematic dream, by design DIVINE. What a plan, man. The breathing LIGHT by Design.
DIVINE LIGHT.

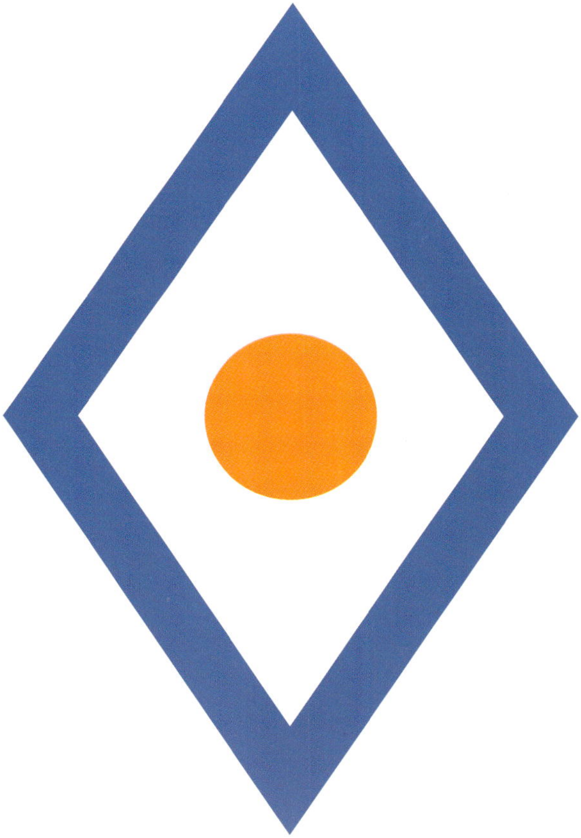

DIVINE KNOWING

Drop the Icons, drop the snowing forgetting, wash your being with the magnificent glowing beam of Indigo pedals sailing full in the windowed spacing knowing that the truth of symbol is at the heart of what matters – at the heart of your heart and healing, piercing, lifting cuts the fog of dogmatic dooming, and there you are – blooming, beaming, knowing – and showing your remembrance in the depths of your balanced return to your dancing feet – eye them, join in, patter the patterns of embracing your knowing – light is shimmering head to toe to eye to soul to spirit bright shining in the middle of your eyes.
DIVINE KNOWING.

Know the trailing, the metallic telling of a gentle stare at the intelligence showing in your light-filled glowing arrival at the lip of the eliptic call DIVINITY'S showing, and in this KNOWING surrender. A laughter is singing in the empirical leaning called DIVINELY KNOWING that life is showing in our telling diamonds of circular spilling. Alice is leaving and the carolling singing met at the web of her lightest leaving is met in our grieving by the letting it go by the gentlest flow, the extravagant show, that intellect and love have met to groove the pieces to fitting completion. Expectant urges and eloquent merges have left me red with reading surrender to the ink in your pencil and the lead in your tip-toeing panic to the edge of this planet. Be glad she's round and know that your running loops are the highest ground meeting your feet with peace-full retreat back to the middle where we long to be Electric and elegant and gentle and blue with indigo red belonging. I am the planet, the Earth and the sky and the intimate longing of a delicate sigh. Gentle the moment and often the match. My singing is ringing in browsing approval of open-eyed centered aligning with the portal of pleasure and tread and upright surmisal of the living we've led, to the inside, the head of the maze, and the delicious taste of a delicate new-age. Creation's ringing with browsing arrival. So long survival, hello regard for the highest living and good-bye the cord of soul striving and endless hiding from your Self, your friend. You are forever, again. Welcome home to the throne of singing praise. God is love and Christos is kind and the Buddha is here to sing a rhyme of lasting rays, of singing seen. We are the One's, the One, the LIGHT. Welcome home. DIVINELY, I AM KNOWING ME and My Basic Humanity.

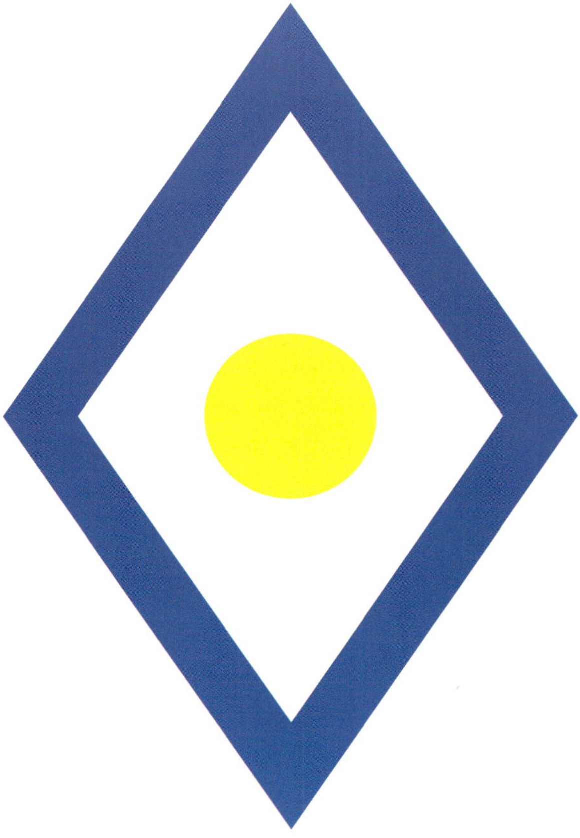

DIVINE BROW-SING

Breaking free of my attempts at deceiving my guiding balanced knowing, I am brow-sing spirit flowing, and I am showing you the toning delight which sharing this magnificent, munificent, swimming sight is like . . .

Sprouting bursts of sparkling opportunity – waves rich and open and freeing like dolphins loving, swimming, homing with humming delight. We are ancient, young, and living examples of divine singing fountains of breath sprouting skyward – foreheads singing and brow-sing Knowing of praises ringing – we are home, we are home, we are free. You are our delight – Our daily One delight. KEEP IT LIGHT.

BROW-SING living is giving me heaps of lifting gaze and I AM lightly led to the top of the tread and the head of the stairs, where the arc of revival is meeting in airs of expression, and ledges of land meet again in the arms of a friend hugging me home, and I AM living a charm of sterling investment and life led in giving living and charming chimes of harmonic octaves of SINGING design. I have arrived at the gap and Darien's been filled and we're walking on tire treads and skimming on lips of edgeless grinning and lapping intrigue at the cups of fresh water expressing their truth – life is in the living, and the giving's in the spin of knowing that your loving is met in peace again, and beauty calls your lovely name 13 times, and absolutely DIVINE you are invited to recline in bliss-full remember of the DIVINEST Design. Musically met by well-come attention to the love-filled compassion of driving it home is a whistling revelation of the dimensional shift. Now we are sailing on eternal embrace of the lifting bliss of all One glorious recline in the arms open wide, our own, by Design. Lightly singing from the heart of our eyes, opening wider to see the river of DIVINE BROW-SING flowing by, we are absolutely aware and filled with surrender to the miracle of vocal confluence – the melodic expansion of intricate inhalation, the voice of this nation, LIGHT. DIVINELY sung.

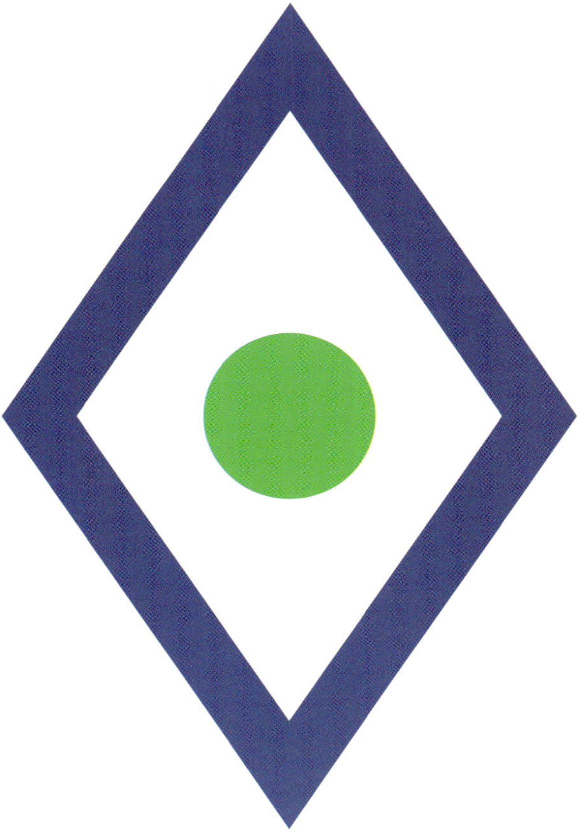

DIVINE ATTENTION

Attention to the detailed appearance of your delightful ship sailing into the harbor of my intentioned, well-embraced seeing eyes – I blink without knowing Other than absolutely this moment. Without fearing diminishment of the sentient sightfull awareness, I give and receive honor and embrace the moment-to-moment excitement of gentled focus on the middle ring of this thrice ringing circuit – remember, attention, remember and knowing this, knowing you, I am electrified and embraced and swollen with penetrating layers of Divine Attention.

ATTENTIVE, I AM, and loving my friend. Know now the power of this Metatronic friend, the office of the Christos has widened the rip and the veil now removed has offered a trip to the Light of forever and the milkiest way, the Light of DIVINITY is home now to stay in perfect rekindle of the delicate aim to float in the lotus of a 1000 eternal names. Hear them well and live to tell the impulsing joy of wisdom showing on your glowing face, melting the depths of your womanly hips and lifting the widening, the hara of breath. Your belly is living and breathing the grip. Let it go. Know the essence of abdominal bliss and pay full ATTENTION to your breathing release and your filling again. You, my friends, are lending ATTENTION to your breathing existance. Know the bliss of the living kiss – your every breath that crosses lips and nostrils flared to breath full lungs of Light. Know the bliss of DIVINE ATTENTION to your breathing rendition of the creator found in the form, daily mirrored, and walking around. Clearly intent to lend attention to my DIVINE dimension. Breath by breath by breath. DIVINE ATTENTION.

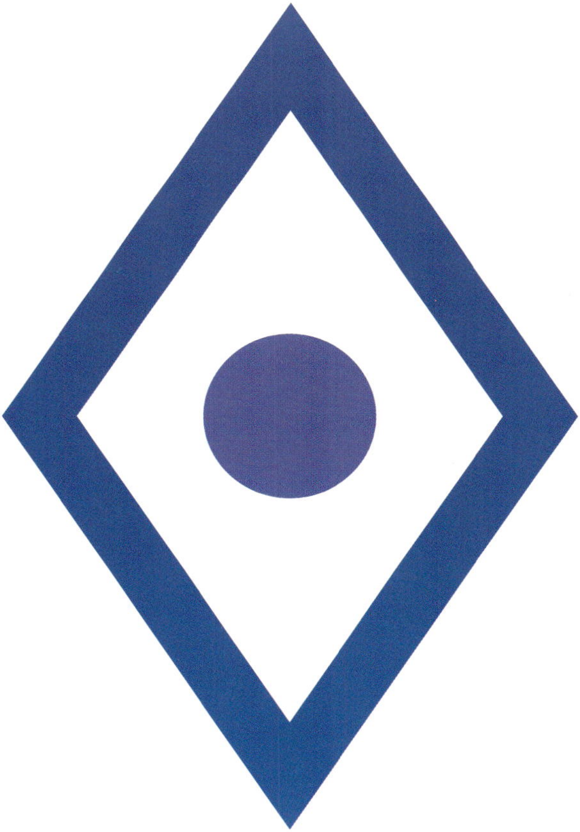

DIVINE INTENTION

Clearly this ringing is singing my crystal clear intention to mention that you are the Way and the Light and the Truth and in this matter it is that which I scatter lightly upon your planet. You are loved and led by the gentlest hand — Trust what is showing. Trust your knowing. And knowing this truth you are Intentionally free. The key is in your seeing inside, in our being ignited with the Intent to set your loving light-hearted self vibrationally and Intentionally free.

DIVINE INTENTION.
Lights the flame . . .
Spread the word . . .
Light.

INTENDING to live in a delicate bliss, I AM led to recline in the love I call mine and left to the middle. I am right to refine my surrendering be-ing to living in-line. Right to a moment I know the repair of living the life I call dancing mid-air. And spinning within I melt my reply to a crystalline matrix and a herkimer sigh. Know the expanse and the ecstasy within of the blissing retrieval of the lighten-ing spin. Lift your INTENTION and hold it in hand. See the clarity of the purity within and knowing the truth, life is full sooth in a tantalizing pleasing dynamic design, designated to win by freeing our will. I am refined to imbibe in perfectly clear watery extremes of lifting my vibe and eliminating the web of forgetting lines. My denial's on trial and the verdict is in. I'm living again. Light's my friend. You are kind to read this line and infinite the plane, this designing called man. Bet the tree is the living me. Mer-ka-bah led and leaving dread to burn with the cross of the eternally lost – good-bye karmic tread. Welcome the light of the eternal life – lived as love by God's own hand, the married man is the One who knows his living shows in his finest power the intimate hour of DIVINE integration. Male and female meeting to meld into one glowing knot at the eye of the Sun – meeting at the trunk, the branches are One – the knotting's done, I AM One, gender-less and living-more, in my ecstatic blend called the Lord of All arrival. Good-bye survival. I AM by DIVINE INTENTION.

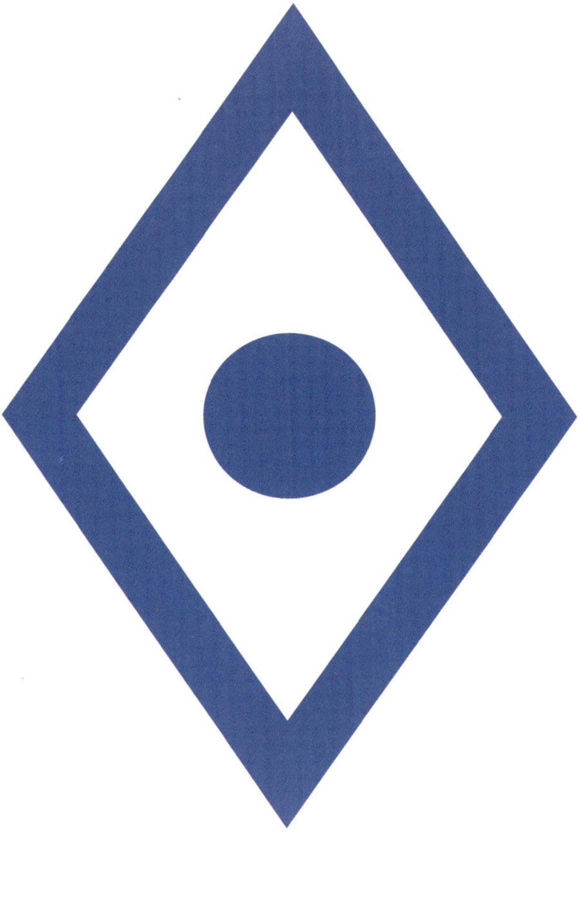

DIVINE INTEGRATION

Entering gracefully the beloved spirit's timing, turning inspiring, enrapture, patterns of forgotten, darkened emission are lifted full against the light and I Am held bright in the shining discovery of places where "less than" meant separation and "other than" meant you'd leave, and "if then" meant of course you'd go and I was shattered and apart and I remembered the spark I AM and I'm off the lam and I'm graciously bowing to the singing way you are ringing me to the delicate edge of letting me find the pieces and tying them smoothly knotted to the edge of an endless Summer's wintered autumn – I spring fully elected, honored and enter-ed gratefully into DIVINE INTEGRATION.
Knowing ME.

Listen up, the living's come. Here's the delicacy's run called the width of your tongue – lacing delicious and watering your breath is the essence of you, the breathing wealth. Where is your ear? Lend it dear, and know the balance of your listening appeal, the tingling sensation of expressive zeal. I like the love and the integrity of faith – your living example of life's flowering blend, the emotive example of essential zen, living LIGHT, simply said by the kindest bite, the tempting taste of a precious plenty melted indigo with a polarized bluing added monographically and unilaterally bent to bend in the middle of fishing for moonbeams. I'm streaming across the face of infinity to lay down the cross of forgetting. My hair looks sublime in the height of my passionate surfing refinement to the width of a curl and a fragrant bouquet scented raspberrial and chamomile, calmed to a tasty arousal of the expectant hush of a biting surmisal . . . life is good. Light is well within the swell of my DIVINE INTEGRATION.

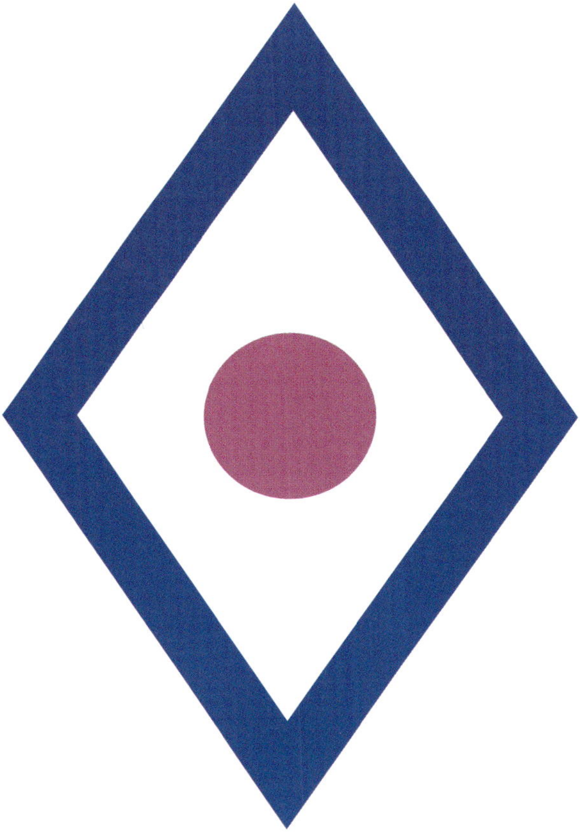

DIVINE I AM

Divinely I AM and uniquely I AM and honestly I AM and in that place is the piece which held me separate and apart and distinctively without myself. I AM and that I AM is the absolute singing, winging, ringing, Absolute deliverance from my little disconnected self. I AM your divine, you are mine, spirit is the light sparkling green and gold and pink and purple and red in silvery-violet flaming return to the eyes of the One . . . I AM. Peacefully, lightly, and tenderly may I share. Gently, wisely and deeply infinity to infinity, arc to heart, heart to hand, light to life and light to spirit. Spirit we are in it and we are full of the DIVINITY of Knowing the I AM in the center.

I AM DIVINE and expressly unique and the one central portal of all of my seek. And I AM content to spin a new web of catching myself and my delectable parts and reeling them in to my great central heart – and loving the man, and loving the woman of faith-full delivering, kind and true to my living, and gentle besides, I AM DIVINE and know the tribe of the communal kind. Kind to a brother and a sister and aunt. I am the square humming circling chants of "I love you sister", and I AM relieved by your sharing state. Save the Sudan by experiencing bliss and sharing your energy with just one kiss full-electric right on the space, the gap in your giving and the electronic taste light metallic ignites deep within, and I know the magnitude of the DIVINITY I AM, by Design, and Well-Aligned with the Living Light, I AM . . . DIVINE.

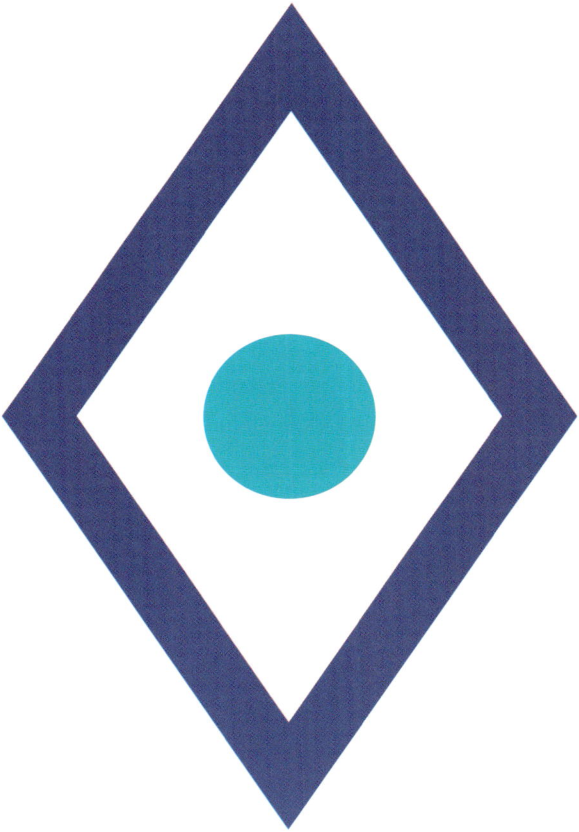

DIVINE MEDITATION

Chanting and singing I AM winging home on the beam of my praising lifting indigo-gold dreaming. Life is light and I AM in it singing my name. Embracing the light of the divinity I AM means I am singing and sounding and breathing and waving and dancing and jamming with the cosmic concentrated, eternal, freeing, resounding sound of the peaceful, empowering showering sound of sounds – my magical name. Light, love, compassion, inspiration, guidance, God, divine, delight design of this minute, this looping return to infinite seeing is ringing in the syllables, the vowels, the constant consonants of my mantra, my chant, my DIVINE MEDITATION – my Best FRIEND – Divinely ME.

MEDITATE on this . . .

The temple called ME is clear through my DIVINE attention to the Light I AM, and my living believing in the DIVINITY of me, the Living Tree. Light's love shining free, and life, is relative to my constant attention to the daily mention of the name most holy, my own, 13 times. Feel the Light, pink and green and lavendar's ametrine renewal of LOVE'S constant vibration . . . 3.14 and add one more, you, to the infinite core – a Light Pyramid. Melting denial. Here's the Revival. Lightly me, to the infinite power, LOVE by DIVINE DECREE. Let there be – ME.

THE DIVINEMENTS

KEY CODES 49 - 56

DIVINE ON-LINE

DIVINE DESSERTS

DIVINE COMMUNICATION

DIVINE NON-MIND

DIVINE SYNCHRONICITY

DIVINE TIME

DIVINE ESSENCE

DIVINE DIVINE

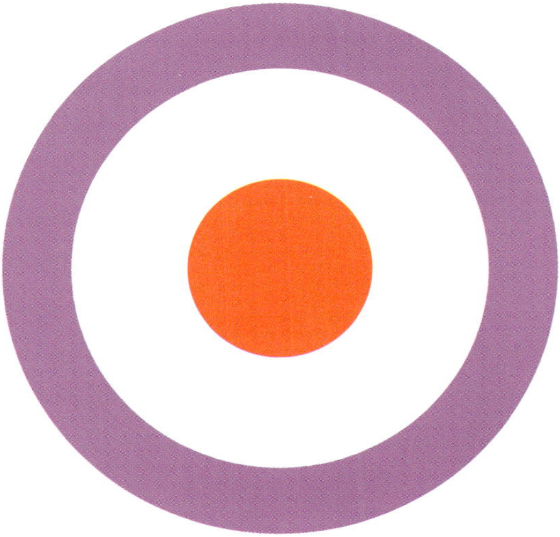

DIVINE ON-LINE

Line up, log on, learn the transcendent truth, pursue the design of the greatest creation, the super-computer, the finest Be-ing, living breathing invention and intention. The point is this moment, skate the rhythm, the rhyme, the schematic dynamic. Learn the lessons, take flight - chat with the light. No need for back-up, for purchasing extra space – the memory – you are in it – a flowing endless river of looping infinite channels of crystalline transmission. Access the balance, write your own allowance, slip into the splendor, surrender the splinter. You are whole and your feet see it and your fingers feel it and the mouse in your pocket clicks on-line divinely on-time.

Tap on the top of the clicking mouse, the vibrating house called the temple I AM, and the lifting example of the kindest blend is the process called living and the timing of sound instrumentals beaming a trim, erecting a flare on the point of the rim of beginning and the delicate swim of a trickling trim of starry revival at the spin of a planet meeting her window of opportune instinctive. Know the proof of the living fall, the watery edge of a sky born green with tradition and webbed with the voice of a singing example of a printed view. You are the computer and the kindest of Kin, the love of a nation and the life of a short introduction and a life starry-eyed and a trinity born of a lightening load. Know the design of a web built to shine and you'll know the lord of electronic sort. The peace of a principle without any cords. Gain the retreat of a life more replete at the ON-LINE DIVINITY called living this time. Know the honor of a grinning daughter, a kinder sun, a living One near the edge of a metallic run – coppery feathered fun to the end. Hawaii is calling like an intimate dream. Wake up the lifetime of a shining example, the sun in your center is singing the breeze of a palmy night glittered with the healing trees. Know the Light of an electric night. We are One. DIVINE to the web of a sight signaled sunny to a fresh design. I AM the Light DIVINELY ON-LINE.

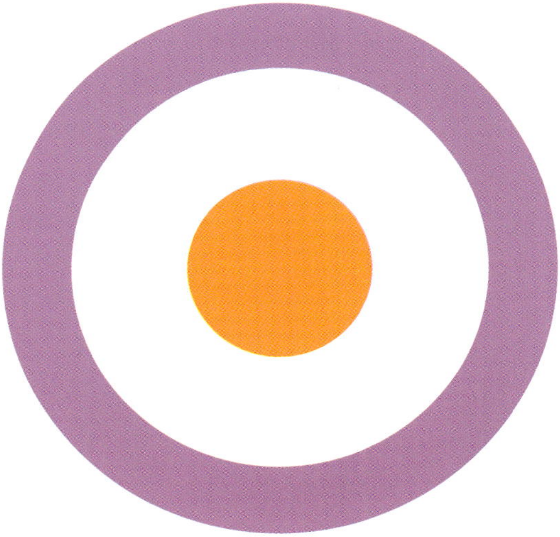

DIVINE DESSERT

Hungry, I AM Filled. Flooded, I AM thrilled
with the delicious remembrance of sweet savory
countenanced beloveds singing round me. You
astound me with your infinite capacity for lulling
me home with the kindest humming admission
that my sweetness fills the dessert, lights the forest
of your lonely living and we are spirits winging,
touching down in the divine dessert of our
towering, standing bones. Trees are ringing.
In their sanction, let us anchor lights of being
returned. Trees are singing, standing people for
our remembering, for our surrendering, building
forests for the tendering of divine desserts – open,
welcome, wet and lush. There is a hush.
Stars are winking across the dessert of my Soul.
Lead me home.

Just in time for a delicate switch, I flip on the light to a much higher nitch and I tremble in ecstasy at the bridge of a sight – a life more dynamic and full of the flight. I am alive now and feel the relief of life in the center of an exotic intrigue. Islands of sunshine employ the wealth of vitamins C and A to the depth of a heart singing engagingly on the plains of the wind of eternal nations examining truth. Blessed the peace-full and ecstatic, the friends of a lofty revival called living again. Enjoy the triumph of an oasis of care creating DIVINITY in the dessert of staring agreement that the Light has begun to sing a new song at the wedge of the One cake so creamy – the floating escape to the island of generosity and the life of intrigue and the love of a lifetime blooming soft on the sleeve of a yearly return to your monthly express of the genuine embrace at the lift of the web, the matrix survival has met the arrival of forever again. Know your friend at the line of a welcoming sign. One island's cure. One season's shore at the brink of a classic relief. Examine the tread. We all know the web of One glorious rest in the arms of the All-mighty forever-ing ways, straight to the middle of a cosmetic way, the cosmic day, an eternal night, an intricate thread unraveling the web of a sail set forever to the sublime shore – the waving center of the island of forever called DIVINE DESSERT.

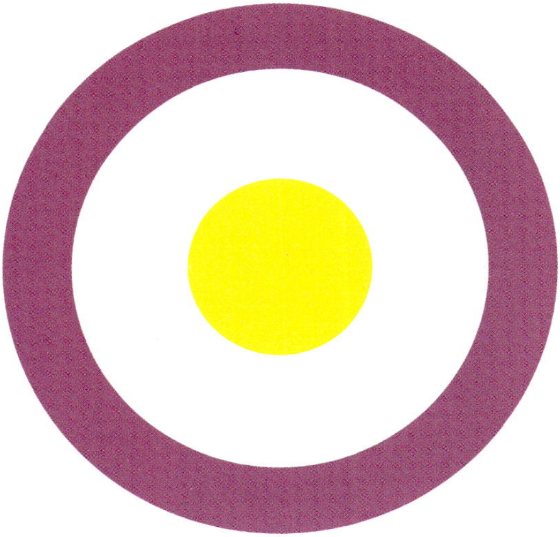

DIVINE COMMUNICATION

Kiss the lip of a night now remembered, dip your pen, just the tip into a surrendering tender light, NOW you're in it and just a minute ride the light stream, feel the ring in your heading, footloose into the being space within the center and you are significant and you are in it and we are filling your being with remembering the trance-cendant. Filled this minute without limit, without thinking, soul is drinking richly fed, souls are red with desiring pulling crystal clear embrace, drawing home the delight, souls are pink taking flight, spirit's leading, seals are opened, life is floating in the light, this tender night of sweet surrender. Fill the union of Sweet Communication. WE REMEMBER.

DIVINE on the line, I am led to incline my ear to hear the whispering sound of life coming down in wavering photons and gesticulating ions of increasing orbit. It's your light, absorb it. Life is calling. A brand new feeling, Life is healing West to East the green and red of loving surrender to passion led. All One Life, One Light, One Sound of light coming round to chat for a bit and rest on the tune called listening, sharing, and COMMUNICATING well my DIVINE INTENTION. Have I mentioned how excellent you are and how welcome by far to the intimate edge called this life giving wedge? Pi's inside and I am resigned to rest this time, this dotted line in circular ticks and clucking strips of chattering stillness and elegant wellness. Eloquent we are in our deserving star led truth spreading circling design of split infinity's returning to soar direct to the source and delicate to here and hear and here – right here in the ear-balancing trio – the heart of my ears hears you straight to the heart of this matter. Me, and You. We COMMUNE in our DIVINE COMMUNICATION, with our breathing word, logos, let it be, DIVINITY, me, light, you. Understand the DIVINE plan in the eternal void of DIVINE COMMUNICATION.

221

DIVINE NON-MIND (VOID)

Soft on my mind, led out of time,
non-existent, void, I am in it, wait a minute
DIVINE NO-THING NO-RING of surrounding,
binding, limit. VOID I am in it. Floating lightly,
softly touching, life is shining, sparkling crystals of
containerless full-feeling, precious pearlescent,
purest floating particles of purple hue. Tanzanite
clouds peopled purply-pink with passionate
embrace of the knowing, sounding we are Arcing
home in a mindless rush, welcoming home in
a singing hush, breathe the moment, smell the
feeling, hear the telling, love is swelling, no-thing
is present and in the void I find my planet, my
home, my life and my heart. Welcome home.
DIVINELY LOVED.
OUT-OF-MIND. OUT-OF-TIME.

Pass the ball at the floating edge and dive on in to the lifting wedge. Examples are set by the courage of light encouraging your visit to the love of this sight. I AM embracing my excellent taste of the genuine design. Where is the attraction of thinking all day and to operating alignment with the petulant kind of grieving forgiven and honesty aligned with the triple contribution of a blessed sign? The light is in the middle and the truth is in the care of an ecstatic appeal called the blending pair of a shaken and stirred windy clearance of foggy forgetting. Welcome the light of a new day's singing. Light here is ringing the empty, now full, life I call you. Love to the limit-less edge of eternity's web. All One in the sun of an eternal day. Light's DIVINE NON-MIND. Void to the lip of an Absolutely full cup. Love. Light. Led to a delicate rhyme called DIVINE NON-MIND.

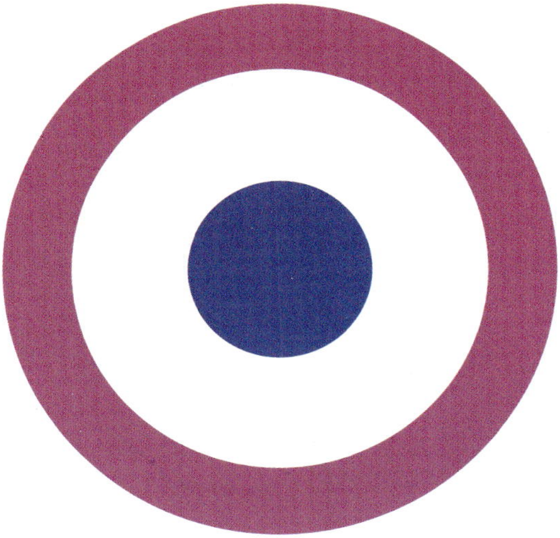

DIVINE SYNCHRONICITY

Time out-of-time, time on a line meeting
lines arcing into the slim, slightest margin and
there you are again and I am in the understanding
that this landing together has no significance
other than to tell us again. Lights are twinkling,
heads are turning. Was that you, who without
warning, drove right in just on loop to scoop me
up, to fix my flat, to know that I am you and in
this Knowing, true, we are One living on time for
two and often it is three and the lines form new
patterns, looks like stars sprinkled light on the
surface of the beneath of the heavens of your eyes,
Knighted skies, ancient wonders. See the splendor.
Know more Splinter . . . less is taken. More is
shaken. More is showing. Meet the flowing.
DIVINELY SYNCHRONOUS
. . . ON TIME.

The perfect presence of an Absolute twist sublime to a second and feeling the fit of shiny attribution and constant access to the precise moment that love has been sent to tender the render of a jubilant stare at the moment's arrival and the emphatic glare of a delicate moment sent to the fair estimation of a dancing wave, the hula girls moving in hypnotic waves of palm trees ecstatic and glistening days of happy arrival at the head of the stairs . . . at the night called today and the love I call ours. Know the power of the DIVINE light, led by design to the living light, grace-full on the face of a lifting sign and a time blessed by DIVINE SYNCHRONICITY.

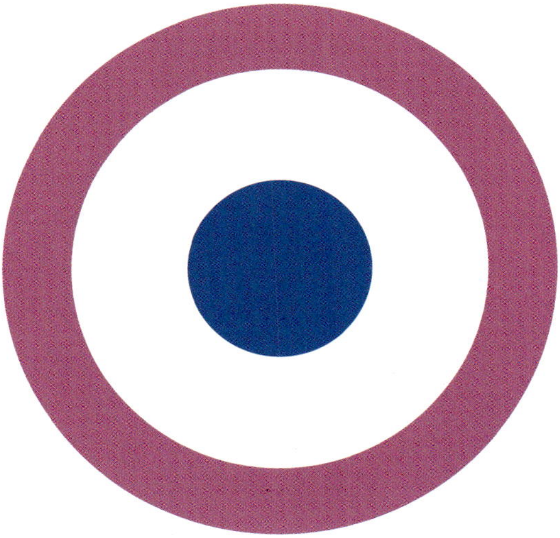

DIVINE TIME

Time after time, I am led to recline in the sublime, the delicious, the oh yes you offered, and the Ah ha you proffered, and the Abha* at center delivering the splinter to the glitter which shivers in simmering delight at the white light blown open to the hallowed sight of spirit emerging, breathing life to the heart, to the place in the middle where All life must start and peace-full in slumber and anchored in light your High self comes sailing enraptured in flight and delving in loving and laughing in gathering, I am melting the forgetting and easing the pain and your whole self steps forward and wholly one lover you are waved with the thundering heart filling sight of the light shining brightly in the depth of the night.

Abha – The center of the heart for all people on earth. Where heart and breath meet.

Stars on the fabric and trees on the edge, I see the web of a matrix led by relative space, tasting like heaven and feeling like Mars, tight in the middle and expanding to stars of excitement and the breaking of gentlest absolution with the loving care of precise inclusion of the living line – the web of proof at the head of a life next to infinity and a loving precise to the center of a given advise. Life's on the line, love is kind, the Earth's our friend, and the Lightening edge is the ultimate sign of a forever blend of DIVINE TIME. You and Me. DIVINE and free. Right on time. One at a TIME. All One Kind. Line by line and square to the circle of a second sign. Loop by loop. An Infinite line. Meeting DIVINE in a wrinkle called TIME. DIVINE and sublime, DIVINE TIME.

DIVINE ESSENCE

Harmoniously sensing the fact that we are breathing reminders of the delicate entwining, I turn softly to the point and the place, that dimension in space where just a dipper of me added to a scoop of you equals that mingling of essence called star's dusting the fabric with brushes of lights – and the spark that is in you ignites combustion in me and I am inspired and set free to dance in the us, the spirit of the dance, and you lead and I lead, consistently led by the flame burning within and the flame's budding shower of creative sparks ignites the light in each Other's eyes and we are completely One and loved and led and Sung. Shine ON.
DIVINE EFFERVESCENT. ESSENCE.

Breath by breath I AM met by tiny slivers of telling ecstatic, by loving tools, given absolute balance – and you are on time in your shining glare and your infinite embrace of the feeling pair, the telling web, DIVINITY's bed – filling the air with an absolute pair of One gentle sun, breathing All night in the light of a sight called breathing relief and the knowing peace of infinite design. Life is sublime here on this fine, multi-tiered taste, the living kind, DIVINE ESSENCE.

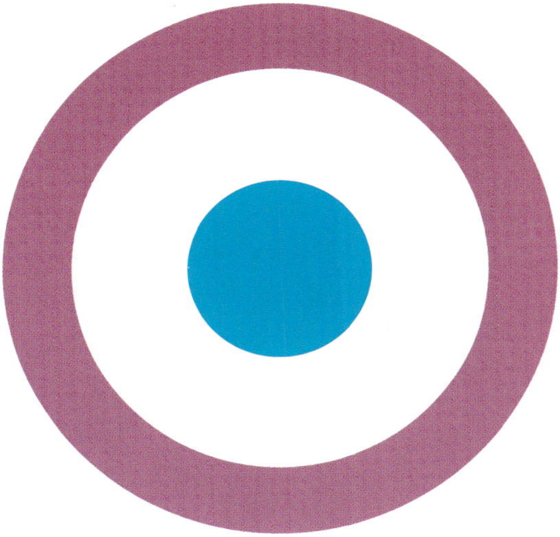

DIVINE DIVINE (WINGS, SEEDS / DANCE)

Lately I am led to intimately discover my ability to recover the elements and essents, the wings and the seeds, the dancing delight of entering divinity's remembering divinity. Essents are God sparks, the pieces of the infinite leading us to infinity and back and beyond, and in front of the middle, life-centered I stand. Enraptured, enlightened, in loving I stand. In joy, in blissing, in Loving I tap and tag I am it, the Divine, the deserving, the best. And I offer myself whole-y to the dance of the Divine tapping and touching and tagging what is mine. What part calls you forth? What is divine? All that I AM, All that you are, and divinity dances at the arm of a star singing at the sight of a Divine holding, Divine dancing life in the spirit of the light.
DIVINE DIVINE.

Thank you, mahalo, and gracias too. The light I kindle is the living proof that this is the line, the human kind – basic and humane, and hand in hand the loving creation, the light called a man. Breath by breath. A woman's in-sight is her elegant breath, the living LIGHT. By design. DIVINE DIVINE.

THE DIVINEMENTS

KEY CODES 57 - 64

DIVINE HUMANITY
DIVINE AUTHORITY
DIVINE ENERGY
DIVINE BELL
DIVINE BIRTHDAY
DIVINE MARRIAGE
DIVINE AUTHORITY
DIVINE IN - LIGHTENMENT

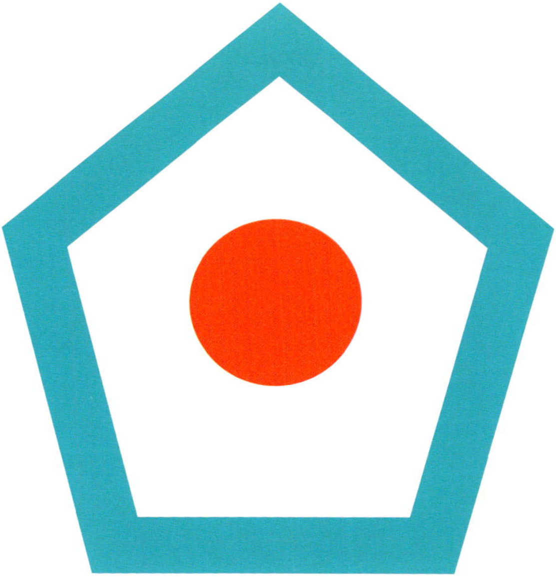

DIVINE HUMANITY

Divinity is delicious and oh, yes it's sweet.
Add in a body and the creation is complete.
Your mission, accepted, is to remember your
union. Sometimes remember, all times intend to
give constant homage to the spirit's light within.
Here is the balance, the harmony, the sight of
connection with heaven shining bright on the
night of a morning forgotten recalled by the sight
of an arc in the heavens playing notes of delight
and full in surrender you are basic and human
and divine and enchanted and one galactic
humanity enthralled by your shining faces
burning soft in the light. This night the winds
are swirling, the sky is twinkling clear, the
messages are coming – DIVINITY spoken here.
LOVE THY SELF and your BASIC HUMANITY.
Spread the word.

I AM HUMANITY'S kindest friend, the Lightest example of an infinite frame. Know the name of a kind of refrain, a sentient state, an excellent taste of a particular vine. An exciting line of living fine to the center of a lusting web – the quilt called HUMANITY – and the blessing called a man – and I know the truth of expressing the plan by the plenty-full expansion of an occupational truth. Life is the name, love is the gaming employ of the power absolute, knowing you, knowing me. DIVINE HUMANITY.

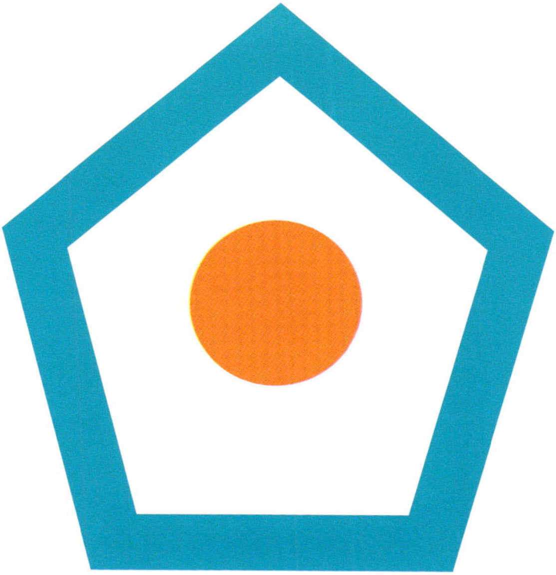

DIVINE AUTHOR

Write your story on the smile shining soft
on your face. Show your delight at completing
this telling, this race. This minute you are in it
and you are loving and free. Tell me, tell others,
enjoy your moment. You are the father, the
mother, and friend and in your delight let the
living begin. Love's spreading wide. We are
welcome and free to dance and delight and to
swim in the sea of remembering bliss and the
sharing embrace of delightful divinity shining
forth from your face. Your eyes tell a story.
Make it no mystery. I love you. I revere you.
I see you in me and in this beloved, spiraling, spin
our hearts wide, ignited burn whole sun and free.
Breathe the beginning and middle and end.
And now is the point where your light's work
begins. LIGHT ON. DIVINE AUTHOR.

I write this life by a tempting sight – my own heart's winging return to the journey, my own, and the circling return to the spinning orb, the heart of this song written along the elipsis of an arcing flight. I know this place and this lifting place called my smiling face. Know this graceful harmonic, the end of the Karmic, and the loop fully owned, your own, by DIVINELY written decree. I AM the Light and the DIVINE AUTHOR of this life. Know the print, it's fine and mine and on-line. Print it. DIVINE AUTHOR ME. Write your plan. Draw your map. Lead the light edge home. DIVINELY written. We are the Light shining bright in our daily news. DIVINE AUTHOR.

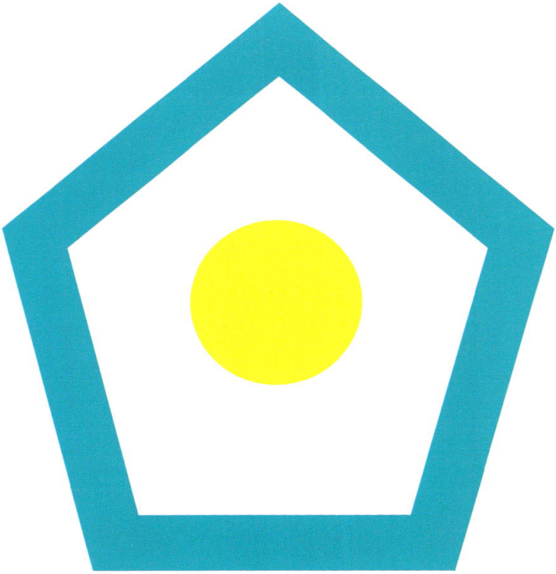

DIVINE ENERGY

Kindly lean into the anchoring bolt of lightening jolt as Kundalini life reaches forth to meet and to greet the being in flight. Above the magnetic there's an ocean electric – select it and ride the waving, terrific board of trusting, merging, infinite light. We are in flight and in the light of a patterning eclectic selectric. Energy is speaking and tweeking the earth link which runs through your core. Today it is you, the divine, the Madonna, the whore – you are my sister, my lover, my brother – and we are the answer to the question within. Join me in lifting, in singing, in joining voice – today is the day when we all see the light at the end of our rope, at the end of the handle – the light's shining bright in the middle of the heaven of your hearts tonight. Ride the swell. DIVINE INNER-G'S.

ENERGY equals me by an infinite LIGHT.
Express the pain, expose the flame and let the healing
complete the ceiling, star to star, at an integrated pace,
an ambiotic float in the sea of DIVINE ENERGY.

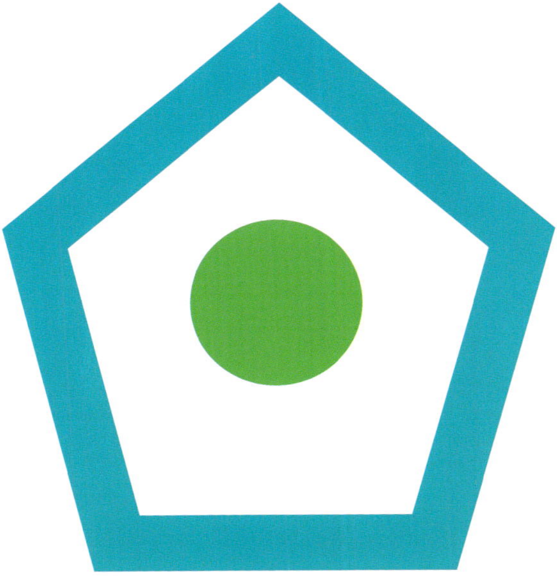

DIVINE BELL (RINGING TRUE)

Grasp the handle and ring it well.
Your divinity is in your hands and you are
wearing it well. Oft times I'm believing you have
a star by the tail. And in my consternation, my
musings on creation, I grasp the constellation
which gives me rise to lift and love with passion
eternal – We are the DIVINE and the creator's
greatest heaven – Look in my eyes and let me see
the light burning whole in the center tonight.
Take a trip. Strip off the chore, life is laden
heavy, lay down your load. For there's a light
shining bright at the end of this flight and its
heaven and earth and abandon and home.
Loosen your belt, toss out the chute, no looking
back, you've finished that loop – standing in
infinity, diving right in. Surf's up inside and I am
ringing this bell. TRUTH'S INSIDE IT.
HEAR IT WELL.

Appealing pleasing knows the squeeze of a moment's notice into a ton of ouncing lightness. Feel the praise of a lifting screen, lose the filter of a delicate flicker, recognize the entreaty of a pleasing plan. Life is aglitter with definite trends for ringing pleasure and answering swells. The seals are all broken and hear is the score, the ringing reminder that the clackers unbent and this bell is repealing the previous trends. God's in the center. Know more inside, and find the spaces of loving retrieval, straight from creation, the strength of a nation blessed to receive the love of a lifetime, a crystal clear tale, of the broken emotion of past, treading motion. Running in place never led to flight until now and then again, you, ringing in the middle, singing the peal of the DIVINE BELL. DIVINELY SINGING. Praises are ringing and my heart sings. Love remains and lights the day of an eternal dawning. The Light is on. Welcome Home. Ringing true. DIVINE BELL.

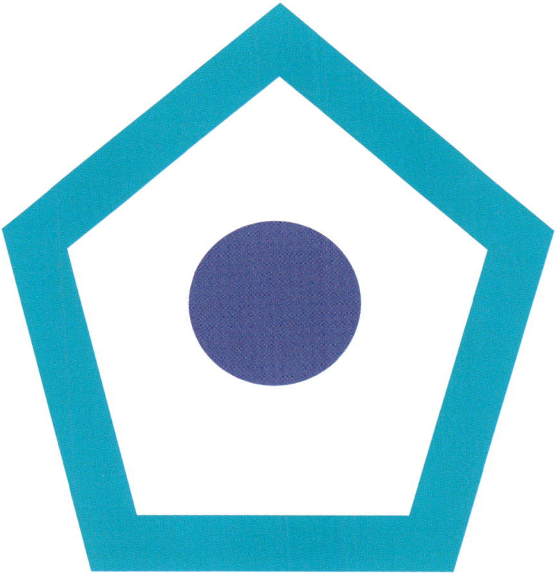

DIVINE BIRTHDAY

My call came in on the heart line tonight, and I am spending these minutes on quarters of being in it. My heart is breathing beauty and love and truth. You my beloveds are our living proof. The heavens are arcing with guiding delight, in the knowing that Arc-ing greetings are heard here tonight. Your birthday is here. Allow us to celebrate the Divinity of your bounti-full-light. The light's shining forward on this planet tonight, reflecting through heavens of welcoming sight. You mirror our believing in no longer deceiving, in no longer hiding the light in your basket. Grasp both handles firmly, stand soft on your feet, and dump all your eggs right out on the street. Now tread on the shattered, the mixed up, the broke cause your feet see the beauty in letting it go. Cake's in the oven. Places are set. Candles form a circle to match the stars smiling in your eyes. THEY LIGHT US UP.
HAPPY BIRTHDAY.

Happy BIRTHDAY . . . blessed ringing, the bell of your truth has spoken in houses of spatial pleasing. Fire to a side, I AM complete in my breathing release of all that is left. Good buy Father, excellent Mother, leaving sister, known the brother, meet the infinity of a living realm, sweet in the center and gentle to last in welcome revival of the loving that lasts. Your Own. DIVINE to the bone and the marrow within and the cells and the corpuscles and every muscle. DIVINE to the skin and to the beauty within, Deep and Light and Loving I AM in my weeping retrieval of the beauty I AM, and you are the Light leading home, this gentle man, the LIVING FATHER – not the written span lacking Truth, but the arcing friend whispering in on a note of perfect D . . . DIVINITY, we two. Welcome friend to the Light that lives in sacred proof of the living truth and the open well and the splashing fountain. Our God is a Light and a mountain and a friend. Eternally burning, a living candle. Happy BIRTHDAY by DIVINITY'S plan. Today's the day. Know the presence of an eternal gift. DIVINE BIRTHDAY.

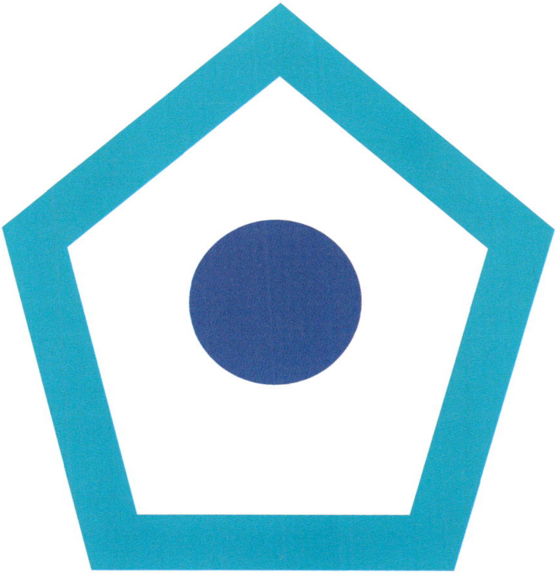

DIVINE MARRIAGE

Rings of reason leaving me replete with questioning glances and quaking earth feet. Making the election, the selection, the choice to marry my living, my breathing, my right with the singing choice left – my heart's bells are ringing. I am happy and whole. Life taking flight. A marriage of inner me to inner you of infinity in me to infinity in you has taken its leap, and we are sailing complete. Take my hand dearest sister, my brother once more let us slumber in a circuit full-filled. The connections sufficient. Your lessons complete. I'll catch you on the upside. I'm projecting a swell. I've let go the ground fear and entered the tube of the ride of this lifetime, of the divinity in you.

DIVINE license is given. Here is your fit. Your birthday is complete and your living is set on the edge of revival and tenting circles of joining rings. Double the pleasure and reveal the truth of the bride inside reaching the place of marrying age. The bull has retreated to reveal a glad fish served on a steamer and lifted to lips of smacking Aquarian bliss. Glad is the spot in my gentle heart's bucket of watery release. I bear the glad tidings, the soul is released, and the ceiling has split to lead home the weary and provide a great lift. The weight has All gone and glory sweet devotion, the living LIGHT is on in me and in you. A DIVINE MARRIAGE by the law of One. We are free in our commitment to the Light I AM. A LIGHT MARRIAGE decreed by DIVINE AUTHORITY.

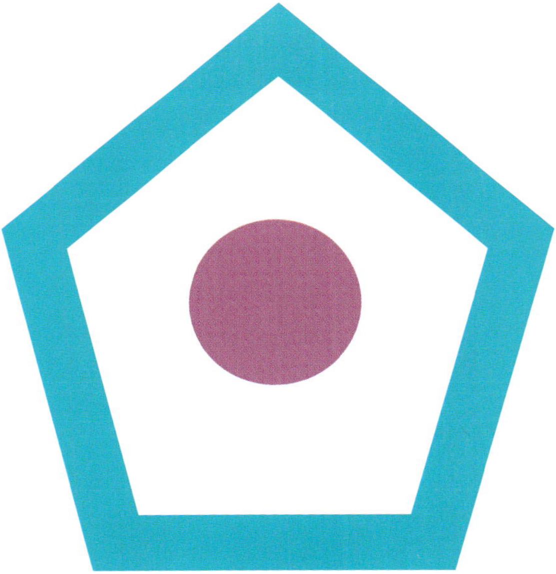

DIVINE AUTHORITY

My dearest heart your truth is told. The hope's in you. Now save your soul. Lift it up in hands of light. Connect yourself to the Arc of life. Humanity needs you. Present yourself fee as a living reminder of your right to fly free. Imagine the potential. Project only truth. Answer right now to the errance of youth. Claim your pieces, destroy the myth. You can start fresh over. Just finish your list. Yesterday is tomorrow in a land far away. Learn from your sorrow and melt it away. Accept that sorrow you created in Other. Ask for forgiveness and extend yet another gesture, more sweet. Welcome to the Light line. You are whole and complete. SHINE ON.

The DIVINE Father, the ultimate gift, the life of an equal
and a song with a riff called heaven is singing in the center of me.
The King-dome I AM is hereby set free by DIVINE DECREE.
Metatron is home and the Light is on. Bless this realm with the
living tree bearing the fruit of metabolic, cystolic, energetic,
shining, ecstatic flight. Only one tree lives in this garden.
The tree of everlasting life in the Light of an eternal Son.
I AM, by DIVINE AUTHORITY. Welcome to Basic Humanity.
The Enlightenment has begun.

DIVINE IN-LIGHT-ENMENT

Divinely a lover of the welcome, the just. Sharing our essence we establish a trust. A trust in the light, that completion so sweet, sing with your ears and smile with your feet. Imagine the finest, the highest, the great. Sing with your brothers and begin to create. Daily give honor. Monitor your juice. The essence of you rides along a new loop. Tonight when you lie down remember that star which spoke in a singing voice, a covenant complete. You are divine and light and free . . . Shining on. We are the Arcs and our meeting complete. Call us sometime on the crystal light line from your hearts to ours for the light's always on and infinite is the power. Divinely speaking , you are the symbol and the light leading home in the space of this life. Tonight lift you homeward and dance in the sparks of the loving surrender at the end of this Arc. Dance lightly upon the planet. You are Divine light shining in the center of this star. SHINE ON.

LIGHT, by nature, knows the balance of body's mind and spirit's incline to live in the form of humanity's charm. Life has a place and an exquisite space, a gentle truth, and a lifting proof. A composite plan is this beauty, a man, a DIVINE design, aligned to the grace of a giving face and an exceptional justice, a truth by the squares, a love sentimental to the circling flair of knowing this skyline, this city, this yard, this Earth's perfect example, the beauty we are, no greater love, than man, by DIVINITY'S plan. Just ask your heart. DIVINE to a perfect spin. Span to span. The Arc that we are, by a holy star, spinning within the glowing LIGHT of our Earthly homes filling sight. DIVINE EN-LIGHT-ENMENT.

Thank you for reading "our" book.
We have many more.
Please visit us at www.basichumanityink.com
or ask for us at your local bookseller.

A special thanks of energetic sort
to the people of Hawaii and her islands
for the inspire called this writing.

Basic Humanity is the complete octave of God
. . . a full scale model of the sound required to be human.

The curriculum for Basic Humanity Ink, Inc. is written in 64 phases, 426 levels. Light. Love. Music. All continuums – with segments written much like minutes of a greater whole – like an hour expressing the multiplicity of a "one". We wish you the lightest choice, called BASIC HUMANITY. The courses offered through Basic Humanity Ink, Inc. are:

PHASE ONE / 64:
THE DIVINE-MENTS
THE IN-LIGHT-ENMENTS
THE ASCEND-MENTS
THE IN-BLISS-MENTS
THE TRANSC-END-ANCES
THE COMMIT-MENTS
THE CONTENT-MENTS
THE IN-PEACE-MENTS
THE PRECIOUS-MENTS
THE PRECISE-MENTS
THE PERFECT-MENTS
THE ABSOLUTE-MENTS
THE SACRED-MENTS
THE COMMAND-MENTS
THE GEOMETRIC-MENTS
THE ARC-MENTS
THE METATRON-MENTS
THE GOD-MENTS
THE ADVANCE-MENTS
THE ENHANCE-MENTS
THE ARCAN-MENTS
THE PROFANE-MENTS
THE PROFOUND-MENTS
THE UNBOUND-MENTS
THE MATCH-MENTS
THE MATTER-MENTS
THE MATERIAL-MENTS
THE BRAND-MENTS
THE BRANCH-MENTS
THE BEFRIEND-MENTS
THE MARK-MENTS
THE PATTERN-MENTS
THE PLAN-MENTS
THE FOUND-MENTS
THE UNIQUE-MENTS
THE GOD-MENTS
THE SANCTUARY-MENTS
THE KINGDO-MENTS
THE SUBATOMIC-MENTS
THE GENETIC-MENTS
THE MOLECULAR-MENTS
THE MUSICAL-MENTS
THE IN-MATH-MENTS
THE METAPHYSICAL-MENTS
THE SUPERLUMINOUS-MENTS
THE IN-PRESENCE-MENTS
THE BLOOD-MENTS
THE GARDEN-MENTS
THE ASSIGN-MENTS
THE AT-HOME-MENTS
THE HUMAN-MENTS
THE TEMPLE-MENTS
THE HOME-MENTS
THE HEAVEN-MENTS
THE BOULEVARD-MENTS
THE IN-STREET-MENTS
THE ASPIRE-MENTS
THE MYSTERY-MENTS
THE MASTERY-MENTS
THE MAGNITUDE-MENTS
THE IN-FOUNTAIN-MENTS
THE FOND-MENTS
THE FOUND-MENTS
THE WELL-MENTS

PHASE TWO / 64:
THE IN-FLIGHT-MENTS
THE IN-FOCUS-MENTS
THE FORWARD-MENTS
THE FACT-MENTS
THE FEATURE-MENTS

THE INFLUENCE-MENTS
THE FUSION-MENTS
THE CYCLE-MENTS
THE CENTRAL-MENTS
THE PORTAL-MENTS
THE PLACE-MENTS
THE POLE-MENTS
THE POSIT-MENTS
THE PLANET-MENTS
THE PORT-MENTS
THE SELAH-MENTS
THE KING-MENTS
THE QUEEN-MENTS
THE PRINCE-MENTS
THE LESSON-MENTS
THE LISTEN-MENTS
THE LEARN-MENTS
THE APPEAR-MENTS
THE APPLY-MENTS
THE EMPLOY-MENTS
THE GAIN-MENTS
THE GRANT-MENTS
THE INFUSE-MENTS
THE FOCAL-MENTS
THE VOCAL-MENTS
THE FORTITUDE-MENTS
THE ENDEAR-MENTS
THE ENTIRE-MENTS
THE ELECTRIC-MENTS
THE ELEVATION-MENTS
THE ATTITUDE-MENTS
THE ELECTIVE-MENTS
THE STAGE-MENTS
THE STORE-MENTS
THE SILVER-MENTS
THE GOLD-MENTS
THE TREASURE-MENTS
THE PLATINUM-MENTS
THE TITANIUM-MENTS
THE ZINC-MENTS
THE CORD-MENTS
THE CUBE-MENTS

THE DNA-MENTS
THE STRAIGHTEN-MENTS
THE EGG-MENTS
THE SPORE-MENTS
THE BIRTH-MENTS
THE IN-SPARK-MENTS
THE ENZYME-MENTS
THE GREEN-MENTS
THE EVOLUTION-MENTS
THE CREATION-MENTS
THE ENDANGER-MENTS
THE HUMAN-MENTS
THE IN-LIFE-MENTS
THE LOVE-MENTS
THE ENCOURAGE-MENTS
THE SOVEREIGN-MENTS
THE ENTITY-MENTS

PHASE THREE / 104:
THE ATMOSPHERE-MENTS
THE SENTINEL-MENTS
THE IN-BRIDGE-MENTS
THE MOVE-MENTS
THE IN-QUADRANT-MENTS
THE REALM-MENTS
THE IN-REGION-MENTS
THE IN-DEPTH-MENTS
THE AGREE-MENTS
THE IN-FATHOM-MENTS
THE IN-CHOIR-MENTS
THE IN-TWIST-MENTS
THE HERALD-MENTS
THE IN-TURN-MENTS
THE IN-MIST-MENTS
THE ON-TABLE-MENTS
THE ENSEMBLE-MENTS
THE INTERIOR-MENTS
THE ENCLAVE-MENTS
THE IN-WORTH-MENTS
THE ANGEL-MENTS
THE IN-OCEAN-MENTS
THE CREED-MENTS

PHASE THREE CONT.

THE IN-SEA-MENTS
THE IN-FILL-MENTS
THE DESERT-MENTS
THE ENDEAR-MENTS
THE IN-WISE-MENTS
THE IN-FASHION-MENTS
THE THIRTEEN-MENTS
THE IN-SEAM-MENTS
THE IN-8-MENTS
THE IN-64-MENTS
THE IN-104-MENTS
THE FABRIC-MENTS
THE IN-D-MENTS
THE HEARLD-MENTS
THE N-TH-MENTS
THE CRYSTAL-MENTS
THE A-MENTS
THE APPROACH-MENTS
THE GENE-MENTS
THE FUEL-MENTS
THE GENETIC-MENTS
THE INITIAL-MENTS
THE RESONANCE-MENTS
THE MATRIMONIAL-MENTS
THE IN-LEVEL-MENTS
THE FORESTRY-MENTS
THE MATERNAL-MENTS
THE PROMOTIONAL-MENTS
THE WEDDED-MENTS
THE IN-BLUE-MENTS
THE TREE-MENTS
THE RIDGE-MENTS
THE IN-TRUTH-MENTS
THE IN-HEALTH-MENTS
THE IN-LUCK-MENTS
THE CONTOUR-MENTS
THE WANTON-MENTS
THE CHROMOSOME-MENTS
THE IN-PLACE-MENTS
THE INDIGO-MENTS
THE MOBILITY-MENTS
THE IN-RED-MENTS
THE MIRACLE-MENTS
THE ORANGE-MENTS
THE MENU-MENTS
THE IN-BUD-MENTS
THE IN-FED-MENTS
THE IN-SEED-MENTS
THE FOOD-MENTS
THE PROTEIN-MENTS
THE NUTRITION-MENTS
THE IN-COLOR-MENTS
THE EMPIRICAL-MENTS
THE IN-SPIRAL-MENTS
THE AFFLUENCE-MENTS
THE EQUINOX-MENTS
THE IN-EARTH-MENTS
THE PRECESSION-MENTS
THE PLANET-MENTS
THE SIGN-MENTS
THE SYMBOL-MENTS
THE FABLE-MENTS
THE LEGEND-MENTS
THE SERMON-MENTS
THE IN-MOVE-MENTS
THE ACCOUNT-MENTS
THE AGILITY-MENTS
THE SPIRITUAL-MENTS
THE MAGICAL-MENTS
THE FINANCIAL-MENTS
THE RELATIONSHIP-MENTS
THE FUNDAMENTAL-MENTS
THE RELATIVE-MENTS
THE IN-CAPTION-MENTS
THE PYRAMID-MENTS
THE JEWELTONE-MENTS
THE MOBILITY-MENTS
THE GEMSTONE-MENTS
THE FULLFILL-MENTS
THE FINAL-MENTS
THE ESSENTIAL-MENTS
THE ENDORSE-MENTS

PHASE FOUR / 64:

If you are looking tonight, for Christos in the sky, approach a star called Arcturus with a singing h-constant and the belief in Humanity which a high self-esteeming extends . . .

THE COHESION-MENTS
THE COGNITION-MENTS
THE COGENCY-MENTS
THE IN-CONSCIOUS-MENTS
THE CONSCIENCE-MENTS
THE CONTAIN-MENTS
THE INCODED-MENTS
THE LOST-MENTS
THE FOUND-MENTS
THE DEDICATED-MENTS
THE EMIT-MENTS
THE OM-MENTS
THE MANE-MENTS
THE PADME-MENTS
THE HUM-MENTS
THE 314-MENTS
THE IN-LAMB-MENTS
THE STELLAR-MENTS
THE STELAE-MENTS
THE IN-STEP-MENTS
THE SOUND-MENTS
THE LADDER-MENTS
THE TRAIL-MENTS
THE IN-PATH-MENTS
THE BATH-MENTS
THE REFLECTION-MENTS
THE ABSORB-MENTS
THE GIVE-MENTS
THE RECEIVE-MENTS
THE IN-CHRIST-MENTS
THE SELF-MENTS
THE IN-HEIGHTEN-MENTS
THE IN-DEPTH-MENTS
THE BREADTH-MENTS
THE IN-MEASURE-MENTS
THE CUBE-MENTS
THE TUBE-MENTS
THE CHAMBER-MENTS
THE TRIANGLE-MENTS
THE ANGEL-MENTS
THE SQUARE-MENTS
THE PROPORTION-MENTS
THE RECTANGLE-MENTS
THE ON-EARTH-MENTS
THE MOON-MENTS
THE SUN-MENTS
THE DAY-MENTS
THE EYE-MENTS
THE PHI-MENTS
THE PI-MENTS
THE RATIO-MENTS
THE SET-MENTS
THE SHELVE-MENTS
THE LEVEL-MENTS
THE STAIR-MENTS
THE IN-FRUIT-MENTS
THE TREE-MENTS
THE FLOWER-MENTS
THE INFORMED-MENTS
THE LEARNS-MENTS
THE REMEMBERS-MENTS

PHASE FIVE / 64:
THE JEWEL-MENTS
THE JOURNEY-MENTS
THE ADVENTURE-MENTS
THE ENIGMA-MENTS
THE CREATURES-MENTS
THE STIGMATA-MENTS
THE STAIN-MENTS
THE IN-WASH-MENTS
THE BLOOD-MENTS
THE LAMB-MENTS
THE SEA-MENTS
THE ANGELIC-MENTS
THE ART-MENTS
THE ARC-MENTS
THE ARMED-MENTS
THE PEN-MENTS
THE HAND-MENTS
THE HELD-MENTS
THE HURLED-MENTS
THE BOLT-MENTS
THE NUT-MENTS
THE UNIVERSE-MENTS
THE SUM-MENTS
THE CALVES-MENTS
THE GOAL-MENTS
THE GLOBES-MENTS
THE GLOW-MENTS
THE HARBOR-MENTS
THE BAY-MENTS
THE ISLAND-MENTS
THE MOUNTAIN-MENTS
THE MUSIC-MENTS
THE BASIC-MENTS
THE SLEEVES-MENTS
THE COATS-MENTS
THE ROOTS-MENTS
THE GENIUS-MENTS
THE PISCIS-MENTS
THE VESICA-MENTS
THE HORIZONTAL-MENTS
THE VERTICAL-MENTS
THE PARALLEL-MENTS
THE 90-DEGREE-MENTS
THE SYNCHRONOUS-MENTS
THE IN-GRID-MENTS
THE MENTOR-MENTS
THE MASON-MENTS
THE ENGINEER-MENTS
THE ETERNAL-BLUEPRINT-MENTS
THE IN-MAP-MENTS
THE CEREMONY-MENTS
THE CELEBRATION-MENTS
THE IN-CHANNEL-MENTS
THE SUPER-IMPOSED-MENTS
THE OVERLAY-MENTS
THE REAL-MENTS
THE ROOMS-MENTS
THE WORD-MENTS
THE FLUID-MENTS
THE WATERS-MENTS
THE PREPARED-MENTS
THE IN-PEARL-MENTS
THE IMBUE-MENTS
THE INTERPRET-MENTS

PHASE SIX:
THE EYE-MENTS

PHASE SEVEN:
THE IN-BRIDGE-MENTS
(Welcome the Buddha)

PHASE EIGHT:
THE HUMANITY-MENTS

PHASE NINE:
THE DIVINE BREATH, THE IN-HA-MENTS

PHASE TEN:
THE ARC-ANGEL-MENTS

PHASE ELEVEN:
THE METATRON-MENTS

PHASE TWELVE:
THE IN-CHRIST-MENTS

CONTINUED...

PHASE THIRTEEN:
THE IN-GOD-MENTS

PHASE FOURTEEN:
THE MARRIAGE-MENTS

PHASE FIFTEEN:
THE TANTRIC-MENTS

PHASE SIXTEEN:
THE ESTEEM-MENTS

PHASE SEVENTEEN:
THE IN-FLIGHT-MENTS

PHASE EIGHTEEN:
THE GOAL-MENTS

PHASE NINETEEN:
THE COMPARISON-MENTS

PHASE TWENTY:
THE HARMONIC-MENTS

PHASE TWENTY-1:
THE OSMOSIS-MENTS

PHASE TWENTY-2:
THE ALGORITHM-MENTS

PHASE TWENTY-3:
THE RENEW-MENTS

PHASE TWENTY-4:
THE OZ-METRIC-MENTS

PHASE TWENTY-5:
THE MATERIAL-MENTS

PHASE TWENTY-6:
THE DEVOTION-MENTS

PHASE TWENTY-7:
THE SALUTE-MENTS

PHASE TWENTY-8:
THE SALUTATION-MENTS

PHASE TWENTY-9:
THE STEERING-MENTS

PHASE THIRTY:
THE CONTROL-MENTS

PHASE THIRTY-1:
THE EM-POWER-MENTS

PHASE THIRTY-2
THE PLURALITY-MENTS

PHASE THIRTY-3:
THE WISDOM-MENTS

PHASE THIRTY-4:
THE EMERALD-MENTS

PHASE THIRTY-5:
THE TABLET-MENTS

PHASE THIRTY-6:
THE ANHK-MENTS

PHASE THIRTY-7:
THE ATON-MENTS

PHASE THIRTY-8:
THE EGYPT-MENTS

PHASE THIRTY-9:
THE IN-REACH-MENTS

PHASE FORTY:
THE ALTAR-MENTS

PHASE FORTY-1:
THE RESPITE-MENTS

PHASE FORTY-2:
THE HELENIC-MENTS

PHASE FORTY-3
THE RAS-MENTS

PHASE FORTY-4:
THE RAVEN-MENTS

PHASE FORTY-5:
THE TRUTH-MENTS

PHASE FORTY-6:
THE IN-TROOP-MENTS

PHASE FORTY-7:
THE IN-DANCE-MENTS

PHASE FORTY-8:
THE SOLO-MENTS

PHASE FORTY-9
THE DEEPENING-MENTS

PHASE FIFTY
THE FALCON-MENTS

PHASE FIFTY-1
THE RESPITE-MENTS

PHASE FIFTY-2
THE IN-REACH-MENTS

PHASE FIFTY-3
THE ROLL-MENTS

PHASE FIFTY-4
THE IN-TURN-MENTS

PHASE FIFTY-6
THE IN-TRIP-MENTS

PHASE FIFTY-7
THE ARC-MENTS

PHASE FIFTY-8
THE ARC-TYPE-MENTS

PHASE FIFTY-9
THE GRACE-MENTS

PHASE SIXTY
THE IN-MUSE-MENTS

PHASE SIXTY-1
THE ELECTRON-MENTS

PHASE SIXTY-2
THE ENERGY-MENTS

PHASE SIXTY-3
THE METATRONIC INSIGHT-MENTS

PHASE SIXTY-4
YHWH
THE IN-HOPE-MENTS
THE MERCY-MENTS
THE GRACE-MENTS
THE FAITH-MENTS
THE COMPASSION-MENTS